Miracle of
SEED-FAITH
ORAL ROBERTS

Miracle of
SEED-FAITH
ORAL ROBERTS

P.O. BOX 34726, CHARLOTTE, N.C. 28234

TABLE OF CONTENTS

Part I
The Three Key Principles of Seed-Faith

1 How I Discovered the Miracle of Seed-Faith and
   How It Works To Meet Needs in My Life Today .. 5
2 The Three Key Principles of Seed-Faith That
   Changed My Life 13
3 How Seed-Giving Can Give You Control Over
   Insurmountable Problems and Help You
   Solve Them 35
4 How My Sister's Seed-Faith Saved
   My Life and Hers 52
5 How I Learned a Lesson Early in My Ministry
   To Look To God as My Source for a Loan 60
6 A Conversation With Jewish Friends
   Concerning Seed-Faith 69
7 How Two Young Men Through Applying the
   Principles of Seed-Faith Became Tulsa's
   Third-Largest Builders 77
8 A Man in a Black Ghetto Said, "He's Just Out
   for the Money." 82
9 The Big Question—Is Money Good or Bad for You? 87

Part II
How Jesus, The Person, Is the Answer to Your Need

10 How God's Supply Always Equals Your Need 95
11 How Christ Appears to You in the Form of
   Your Need 101
12 How a Friend Got His Dream Job Through
   Applying the Key Principles of the Blessing-Pact..111
13 A Vietnam Veteran Asks, "Oral Roberts, What
   Person Do You Turn To When You Are in a Jam?" 116

Part III
Is Your Blessing-Pact Working?
Here's How to Check Yourself

14 When It Doesn't Seem To Work—How To Check
Yourself on the Three Key Principles of the
Blessing-Pact 123
15 How the Spirit of Your Giving Influences
Your Receiving 129
16 Why I Selected and Gave My Largest Bill 133
17 When Need After Need Faces You—
Here's What To Do 139
18 Let's You and Me Have a Heart-to-Heart
Talk That Can Help You 153

PART I

THE THREE KEY PRINCIPLES
OF SEED-FAITH

1

HOW I DISCOVERED THE MIRACLE OF SEED-FAITH AND HOW IT WORKS TO MEET NEEDS IN MY LIFE TODAY

IN THIS BOOK I want to share with you how I came to have positive faith to get my needs met. I discovered the principles that Jesus used, also His apostles and others spoken of in the Bible.

These principles have become so real and personal that they are a way of life for me. I have tested them against every type of need and problem, both spiritual and material, and they work. They have never failed me. When I had no earthly source or person to turn to; when I was alone with nothing but big problems and challenges facing me, these principles showed me God is my Source. They showed me how to use my giving as a seed I was planting, and to expect God to multiply it even if it took a miracle.

These principles became SEED-FAITH to me. Everything starts with a seed.

In the beginning God said that as long as the earth remains there will be "seedtime and harvest" (Genesis 8:22).

St. Paul referred to the eternal law of sowing and reaping in Galatians 6:7, "Be not deceived; God is not mocked: for whatsoever a man soweth, that shall he also reap."

Jesus constantly likened faith with a seed being planted to get a result. He said, "If ye have faith as a grain of mus-

ta; d seed, ye shall say unto this mountain, Remove hence
to yonder place; and it shall remove" (Matthew 17:20).

If you have faith as a seed, or, if your believing becomes
SEED-FAITH, no matter how small it seems to be, it will
meet needs and problems that appear as impossible as moun-
tains before you. This is because each act of faith is a seed
planted and will be multiplied many times.

A COVENANT OF BLESSING

One day in the early fifties while driving down the high-
way in the great Pacific Northwest, I was facing a staggering
problem. The beautiful Columbia River flowed to my left
for several hundred miles and the countryside was alive with
color. Every now and then deer would run across the high-
way in front of me. I was on my way to another crusade and
I wanted this time alone to think and meditate and give the
Lord time to speak to my heart.

I've never been a person who can live with a need. Something has to give — me or the need.

A big need was challenging me that day. I felt so small
and inadequate. There seemed to be no way to meet this
need. On both sides of the road I saw farmers reaping their
harvests. Trucks would pass loaded with wheat.

Passing through the area where the Delicious apples are
raised, I saw refrigerated railcars being loaded to carry them
to markets throughout America. Everywhere I looked nature
was in production. Seed had been planted, the soil cultivated,
and now the mighty reproduction forces had produced the
harvest. It was one of the most striking sights I had ever seen.

I had faith, a lot of it. It had worked for me many times.
Through it I had been lifted from obscurity to a worldwide
ministry to tens of thousands. At times I felt in absolute
control as I felt the faith working in my heart; at other times

6

it was like I had no faith at all. Seemingly I was not able to believe. Needs that I would face with unswerving assurance on one occasion would be, at other times, so formidable and challenging that I felt fear in the pit of my stomach and would be as helpless as a child.

What I needed was to be able to control and direct my faith at all times. Jesus did it. Why couldn't any follower of Jesus do it if he applied what Jesus did? Why couldn't I do this in the NOW of my existence? Like the seed the farmers had planted and the harvest I saw them taking to market, why couldn't I use my faith in a similar way and get results?

As I meditated on this, a thought came crystal clear, *Whatever you can conceive, and believe, you can do!*
It was God speaking in my heart from the teaching of the Bible linking me with His creative power. It was a reminder of the way He created the earth, made man, and instituted a law of sowing and reaping. It was a reminder that He had sent His Son, Jesus Christ, to earth to give man abundant life. All at once I saw that God's conceptual purpose was carried on through faith, not only in the beginning, not only when Jesus was on earth, but in the NOW.

I could feel my inner man begin to stir. I could feel myself standing up on the inside. I became excited as I began to see the meaning of the idea God had brought to my mind, *Whatever you can conceive, and believe, you can do!*

I saw God had first conceived the world and man. I saw He had believed. And what faith it was! God had believed in man enough to create him with the power to choose good or evil, to live positively or negatively, to believe or to doubt, to respond to God or denounce Him. God believed so much in man even when he had gone his own way and sinned, bringing suffering and death into the world, that He sent His only begotten Son to earth to become a man and bring man

7

to the place where he could be redeemed, given a new life, and live abundantly.

I had always been impressed with God's faith in man. That day I saw more clearly how faith, rightly directed, is the key to everything.

Then I saw on the practical level of human need that God has made it possible for a person to conceive, to believe, and to get right results. The vision was all around me; the harvest in the fields bursting forth from the tiny seeds planted months before and carefully tended; the farmer in control of the seeds he planted. The ground he sowed it in was designed to reproduce whatever was sown in it. The inevitable result was a harvest! This is God blessing man. This is God wanting him to live — to live abundantly.

"I WILL CALL IT MY BLESSING-PACT COVENANT WITH GOD"

It came to me with an impact I felt through my entire being: Jesus as the SEED God planted; through Him God conceived every person becoming a new person, living a new life by the higher law of faith. Jesus is God's covenant of blessing for every man. Through Jesus I can make a covenant of blessing with God. I said, "I will call it My Blessing-Pact Covenant with God."

Gradually the picture became clearer. My Blessing-Pact Covenant was based on my faith in Him. Each time I had a need I could make my faith an act of my believing; I could release it toward God. It was a seed I would plant; the seed would be giving something of myself as God had given His Son or "the Seed of David," and through it I would expect God to reproduce and multiply it even if it took a miracle.

The idea of SEED-FAITH was born in my heart that day when I saw that everything God does starts with a seed planted.

Through the years, the terms BLESSING-PACT COVE-NANT and SEED-FAITH have become synonymous with me. I use them interchangeably. There can be no covenant I make with God without faith that He is going to bless me, and there can be no faith without having my personal covenant with God first in my life.

When people ask how we have accomplished the things that we have I answer in a general sense by saying, "By faith." When they ask me to be more specific and explain in detail I usually say, "The Blessing-Pact Covenant through SEED-FAITH."

My warm friend Billy Graham dedicated Oral Roberts University before 18,000 people on April 2, 1967. I had been a delegate to the World Congress on Evangelism in Berlin which Billy had organized. Everything had run so smoothly and the results were so spectacular that I had publicly stated in introducing Billy that day on campus, "I have been 'out-organized.'"

Billy told the great crowd, "After seeing this great University, I want to say I have been 'outfinanced.'" The crowd cheered.

I was sitting directly behind Billy when he said this and I said quietly, "By faith, Billy." Billy repeated it over the microphone and again the crowd cheered.

Although Billy and I were bantering a little, we both knew that whatever we do to help the people begins and ends with faith.

For faith to become workable, however, I discovered that it had to become an act of believing, something I did, and when I did it, I released my faith. (See my book, HOW TO FIND YOUR POINT OF CONTACT WITH GOD.)

In the Blessing-Pact Covenant as it acts on SEED-FAITH, I discovered three key principles. Through these

9

principles I found I could face a need in a spirit of faith rather than doubt. Instead of becoming part of the problem I could be part of the solution. I could see that a need exists to be met rather than existing to harass and intimidate me.

This has been a big turning point in my life. I look upon my needs now knowing that Jesus is at the point of my need. He is there in the form of the need.

It's true I have not seen every need met. Perhaps I never will. But I have discovered a lot of them have been met that ordinarily I would have marked: "These needs cannot be met."

I have learned that when NOW is my problem; when I am hurting NOW, I can say, "Where is the Lord now?" And find Him replying, "I am here at the point of your need." It is an entirely new approach from the one I used to take.

Problems are real. They exist. It seems when one is solved, another presents itself. But I don't have to pretend they don't exist, I don't have to withdraw from life.

In the next chapters of this book I want to cut through to the key issues of things people face today. I talk about people I know, experiences they have had or we have had together, and share solutions based on SEED-FAITH as revealed in the living Word of God.

What I am saying is based on the Bible, not mere humanism or psychology. It is far deeper than positive thinking. It is our Lord at work, demonstrating in His own life and in the lives of these people whose experiences I relate that He is in the NOW.

I urge you to be very personal about the things you read in this book. Insert your own name in some of these life situations you will read. Say to yourself, "How can I apply this to my need, my problem? How can I know Jesus like this? What do I need to apply the principles of SEED-FAITH in

10

the Blessing-Pact Covenant with God? How can I make God real to me in the now?"

Be bold. Seize the ideas that we have proven to be true and workable. At all times keep your eyes on Jesus and realize I am not talking about just a formula or a plan but a PERSON, Jesus Christ of Nazareth, who must become first in your life.

Now discover for yourself the three key principles that will change your life.

"Give, and it shall be given unto you; good measure, pressed down, and shaken together, and running over, shall men give into your bosom. For with the same measure that ye mete withal it shall be measured to you again."

Luke 6:38

2 THE THREE KEY PRINCIPLES OF SEED-FAITH THAT CHANGED MY LIFE

WHAT ARE THREE KEY PRINCIPLES of SEED-FAITH that changed my life? How can they be applied in your life? How do they become SEED-FAITH?

These three principles run throughout the Bible in God's dealings with His people. They are gathered up and clarified by Jesus in His life and teachings. The writers of our New Testament are abundantly clear on them. Thousands in every walk of life today are applying them to their needs and are getting answers.

THE FIRST KEY PRINCIPLE: GOD IS YOUR SOURCE

You turn your life over to God and start looking directly and personally to Him as THE Source of your supply.

Although there are scores of Scriptures from Genesis to Revelation concerning God as Source, the key Scripture is Philippians 4:19: "My God shall supply all your need according to his riches in glory by Christ Jesus."

Living in a man-run society and business community, it is easy to get the idea that man is your source of supply. This is where you miss the truth of God's Holy Word. God often uses man as the means but God himself is THE Source. All other sources are instruments only.

In looking for your needs to be met, remember it's not what is your source, but Who is your Source?

You may think it's man you are dealing with but he is only an instrument. You are dealing directly with God as the loving Being who is THE Source of your supply. By looking to Him, you are confident, you are positive, you are expectant that He will provide.

THE DIFFERENCE BETWEEN SOURCE AND INSTRUMENT

While I was growing up we lived close to an uncle who made his living from his big orchard. In his later life it was my privilege to lead him to Christ. We spent many happy moments together. It was he who first helped me to see the difference between source and instrument.

He raised apples, peaches, apricots, cherries, pears, grapes, berries and several other fruit. His pride and joy was the big luscious Elberta peach. People came from miles around to buy this peach.

When I entered the ministry I moved away; it was several years before I visited my uncle again. I was shocked when I saw the orchard, or what remained of it. Gone were most of the beautiful fruit-growing trees. Only one or two trees of the prized Elberta peach remained. They were stubby and produced only a few small peaches.

"What's happened?" I asked my uncle. "Did you have a storm? Was there an invasion of insects? Where is the orchard — the peaches, and the other fruit?"

He said, "Oral, they're gone. But it wasn't a storm, it wasn't insects. It was me."

I said, "What did you do that caused this to happen?"

Sadly he replied, "I'll tell you what I did. As long as the fruit came each fall, I was satisfied to leave the trees alone. They bore fruit and I thought my supply was the fruit. The

14

fruit fed my family. We sold thousands of bushels for money and used the money. The fruit became everything to me. It was my business. I depended upon it. Everything I did I judged according to how it related to the fruit. Then one year the crop was not so good. The next year it was less. That was when I stopped thinking about fruit and started looking to the trees. Before, I had paid little attention to the trees. I cut the weeds and did a little plowing down each row. Then I woke up and realized that the peaches and the other fruit were just what they were — fruit of the tree. The supply was the tree. If I took care of the tree, the fruit would grow. Through poor understanding and haphazard care of the trees, I have only these few poor trees left. There's not enough fruit to pick anymore."

Then his eyes lighted up. He said, "But I'm putting in a young orchard. I've gone to the agricultural experts and learned how to take care of the tree first. So, I'm starting over. This time I'll take care of my source."

Immediately I saw how I had been doing the same thing. I had looked to results as my source rather than to God who had sent them.

I had failed to see that the various people who had helped me, and the places where I drew an income were instruments, results — not my Source at all.

WHY LIMIT GOD?

When I entered this ministry in 1947, I still was bound by this unscriptural concept.

The board of the church where I was pastoring set my salary. It was so small I couldn't pay the tuition at the university where I was studying. My family didn't have proper clothes; our car needed repairing. Sometimes Evelyn would go to the grocery store and fill up her cart, only to have to unload part of it at the cash register stand where she had to pay for it. It was getting us down.

There I was up before the people trying to tell them about God. I knew they had needs, too. I could triumphantly share God's love for their souls and spiritual welfare and they understood it. When I attempted to apply the Word of God to the healing of their bodies and for the supplying of their material needs, the words would often stick in my throat.

I told how God met people's needs in Bible times, how He was concerned for the total person, but there was no demonstration in my life or the lives of those to whom I ministered.

Then one day I told the board I had figured up the absolute minimum required for me and my family to exist. I included groceries, car care, clothes, even a haircut twice a month. I figured it almost to the penny. It came to $55 a week. They granted my request to the letter.

For the next several weeks we squeezed by until I realized I was limiting God by looking to the board for my supply. I discovered resentment in my heart. Why didn't they raise me? Why didn't they see the needs of my family? With the exception of the hours I spent each week in class, my whole life was engaged with the people of this church. I was on call day and night for sick calls, etc.

One day I saw that the board was not my source; God was. God wanted to meet my needs. I should take the lid off my faith; I should stop praying for the board to give me a raise; I should start looking to Him who promised to supply all my needs according to His riches, not the meager resources of that little church. I should start looking to this group as only an instrument or means God would use. When I faced needs, I should look to God in a direct way and trust

Him to help me through any means He chose.

Gone was my resentment. I knew God could make a way. I knew He controlled all the means of supply, both expected and unexpected.

Sharing this with Evelyn was a great delight. She has always been practical about money matters, knowing it takes so much to raise a family. I could tell the idea of looking to God as our Source inspired her.

We have learned that looking to people is the sure road to disillusionment. The same is often true if they look only to us. When we think that our friend, or our employer, or an employee is the source of our supply, we are dealing with means and not source.

I will have much more to say about this later in the book. But remember, Jesus said, "With men it is impossible, but not with God: for with God all things are possible" (Mark 10:27).

THE SECOND KEY PRINCIPLE: GIVE THAT IT MAY BE GIVEN TO YOU

The many Scriptures on the right use of giving to get your needs met are so numerous in the Bible they would probably fill this entire book. The life-style of Jesus was giving. The key Scripture He gives us for the second key principle of SEED-FAITH is Luke 6:38, "Give, and it shall be given unto you; good measure, pressed down, and shaken together, and running over, shall men give into your bosom. For with the same measure that ye mete withal it shall be measured to you again." Jesus is saying, when we give, it will be given to us. Not only will God give to us, but men, whether they know it or not, will be God-inspired to be generous with us.

MORE PRODUCTIVE TO GIVE

I used to wonder what Jesus meant when He said, "It is

17

more blessed to give than to receive." It seemed so contrary to real life. I received such a blessing when I received something. Our needs were so many that any small gift thrilled us. It was a joy to receive.

Only occasionally did I experience the same joy by giving as I did when receiving. Overall it appeared to me to be opposite of what Jesus said. To me it seemed to be more blessed to RECEIVE than to give.

Then one day I began to see what Jesus meant. While facing a need I had a deep impression that I should give a certain amount of money to God's work. After I gave it, I felt a warm glow all over. It was pure joy. Somehow I forgot about my need until a man knocked at my door at 2 o'clock in the morning. "Pardon me," he said, "but I had to come back and see you."

He had been present earlier and observed my giving. "When I reached home and started to bed," he told me, "the Lord began dealing with my heart. You didn't mention your needs but only the needs of God's work. For two years I had given very little and all at once it came home to me about my own need to give. I don't know why but I had an almost irresistible feeling that I should give this to you."

He handed me a sum seven times more than I had given! It was the exact amount Evelyn and I needed to continue living in the house we were in. This was our most urgent need.

When I started thanking him, he replied, "Don't thank me. I'm a wheat farmer and I know by experience that the yield I get from my land is in direct proportion to the seed I plant."

As he was closing the door he said, "Brother Roberts, this is just seed I've been needing to plant for a long time."

In his heart, this man had been withdrawn from the

church for two years. His seed-giving was also withdrawn. Like the seed-money Jesus told about in the parable on giving, it was "buried." (See Matthew 25:14-28.) He had let his beautiful farm run down. Worse, he had gotten caught up in playing the stock market. He couldn't cope with the fluctuating market on a daily basis and lost thousands of dollars.

After he started his giving again and assumed his proper place in the church, everyone saw a profound change take place in his life. He quietly resumed tending his farm, he found a new joy in being with his family and became one of the most enthusiastic men in the church that I have ever met. He became a man of strength to all of us. He is still a partner with me today. He still practices SEED-FAITH. His last letter was full of praises to God for showing him how to live.

As I reflected on how God multiplied my gift seven times over, I began to realize what Jesus meant when He said, "It is more blessed to give than to receive." I understood that He was saying, "It is more PRODUCTIVE to give than to receive." For what we receive is not multiplied, but only what we give!

Being a Christian is the best deal a man ever had. If there were not a hell to shun and a heaven to gain, the practice of the principles Christ laid down would still make it the greatest life in the world.

I still get excited about this principle of SEED-FAITH. I have discovered nothing that has meant more to people than this: it is more productive to give than to receive. Giving was the life-style of Jesus.

Yet this idea runs counter to the thinking of a great many Christians. This is where I had to change my thinking.

Giving is the logical outgrowth of looking to God as your

Source, of loving Him enough to give, and of giving as seed that you may receive.

WHY IS GIVING NECESSARY?

Every time you breathe, breathing is both a giving and receiving. You must breathe out to breathe in. So is your very life, for stop either exhaling or inhaling and you cannot live.

WHY IS GIVING NECESSARY?

The farmer who plants a crop must give to the earth. He must sow seed; otherwise, he will harvest only weeds. The seed he gives to the earth will be multiplied back to him, a far greater return than the amount planted.

WHY IS GIVING NECESSARY?

Prayer must have the added essential of giving first. What kind of giving? THANKSGIVING. "Be careful for nothing; but in every thing by prayer and supplication with thanksgiving let your requests be made known unto God" (Philippians 4:6). The seed of thanksgiving with your prayer request is an affirmation of God's return to you.

WHY IS GIVING NECESSARY?

Only what you give can God multiply back to you again. Only when the little lad gave his lunch of five loaves and two fishes could Jesus multiply them to feed 5,000 hungry men and give back to the lad 12 baskets full. (See John 6:13.)

WHY IS GIVING NECESSARY?

Money is the medium of exchange. It is you. It represents your labor, your skill, your sweat and effort — your whole self. When you give it, you give yourself. The Bible says, "Ye are not your own ... ye are bought with a price: therefore, glorify God in your body, and in your spirit, which are God's" (1 Corinthians 6:19, 20).

WHY IS GIVING NECESSARY?

Jesus is interested in the multiplication of your SEED-FAITH because it is the multiplication of yourself. Jesus expressed this truth: "A good tree bringeth forth ... good fruit ..."

WHY IS GIVING NECESSARY?

Jesus says when you give freely, joyously, with full measure, then your giving will be multiplied back to you in the same spirit — "GOOD MEASURE, PRESSED DOWN, AND SHAKEN TOGETHER, AND RUNNING OVER" (Luke 6:38).

WHY IS GIVING NECESSARY?

What you give is the seed you plant. And like attracts like. You plant wheat and you will get wheat. Plant peaches and you will get peaches. God says, "Each after its kind." If you want God to supply your financial needs, then give SEED-MONEY for Him to reproduce and multiply. If your need is not money but something else, let the seed you give represent it. Use it as your point of contact to release your faith for God to meet this need.

For example, if you need companionship, find a lonely person (you won't have to look far) and share seed-friendship. The Bible says, "A man that hath friends must shew himself friendly" (Proverbs 18:24). Or give a seed-smile or seed-love or seed-compassion. Just as you breathe out in order to breathe in, you will see these as seed-giving multiplied back in the form of your need. Not necessarily from the person to whom you give, because that person is not

21

THE Source. (I warn you not to expect back from the person to whom you give. It is my experience that usually the individual will not give back to you. Why should he? He is not THE Source.) But God will multiply it back to you in your time of need through the person He chooses. Remember, in SEED-FAITH, God as your Source is a better selector of persons or the instrument to help you than you are.

At a recent faculty prayer meeting in my home, the wife of one of the ORU professors said, "I must share with you an exciting discovery I have made. When Brother Roberts explained that our Blessing-Pact Covenant with God works on the three key principles of SEED-FAITH, I tried very hard to understand. You see, we have seven children. When I have to take all seven to the shoe store, I often find I don't have enough money to go 'round. Some of the children have had to wear shoes that pinched their feet."

We all knew what she meant. She said, "For several years when this happened or when they needed clothes and I couldn't clothe them properly, I would ask God to make the company who employed my husband raise his salary."

I laughed and said, "Yes, and I imagine if the company raised it every time you asked, it could have gone broke. No company can be your source of supply, it is only one means that God uses."

She said, "I've learned that now. But until recently, I expected everything to come out of my husband's check from that company.

"You said 'God is our Source,' and that He can supply in many ways, even from unexpected sources. Well, this helped me to start looking to Him more. I was able to redirect my thinking toward God as Source. And it works! From that time, when it is shoe-buying time, God has always sent us enough money, often in a way we least expected."

She said, "I'm happy to say that my children are wearing shoes that fit their feet; they have the clothes they need."

Now in tears, she said, "Just think of all those years when I didn't know I was to look to God as my Source. You who have children know what it means to them and to you to have them properly clothed and cared for. You should ask yourself as I did, 'To what source am I looking? Am I trying to tell God how to supply my needs?'"

Our Master said, "Consider the lilies how they grow: they toil not, they spin not; and yet I say unto you, that Solomon in all his glory was not arrayed like one of these. If then God so clothe the grass, which is to day in the field, and to morrow is cast into the oven; how much more will he clothe you, O ye of little faith?" (Luke 12:27, 28). Then He said, "But rather seek ye the kingdom of God; and all these things shall be added unto you" (Luke 12:31).

In other words, you don't try to select the person or persons who will be the means of your supply. You look to God, you put Him first, and know that He as Source will add to you the things you need.

THE LAW OF SOWING AND REAPING

The first key principle is to turn your life over to God and look to Him as THE Source of your supply. Because you love God and trust in Him as your Source, the second key is to give to Him FIRST. Whatever you give becomes seed for Him to multiply back in the form of your needs.

It is the giving of talent, the giving of time, the giving of love, the giving of compassion, the giving of money; really, it is the giving of yourself. Whatever the gift, it represents you. It is seed that you are sowing. God accepts it as SEED-FAITH and applies to it the law of sowing and reaping.

God's multiplying back what you give — I call this a

23

miracle. I know no other word for it. Who can explain the phenomenon of a seed growing and multiplying?

Each time I visit the giant redwoods in California I marvel at their size. Hundreds of years ago each tree was one tiny seed. Looking at one tree through which a road is cut and seeing the mighty branches hundreds of feet above, all I can say is, "It's a miracle."

Take the young lad who gave his lunch of five small loaves and two fishes to Jesus. There was no way he could conceive how Jesus would multiply it into 5,000 man-sized meals to feed the same number of hungry men and give an overflow of 12 baskets back to the little lad. (John 6:13.) (There were probably more than 12 baskets left over but apparently there were only 12 people gathering.)

The small seed-lunch became SEED-FAITH when it was given to Jesus. Jesus used it to help others, and then to meet the needs of the lad, whose lunch was, no doubt, too small and probably not sufficient for him. Jesus multiplied not only his material supply but his faith also. Ever afterward, the little boy could remember his faith was like seed. And when he used it, it would get bigger. (See Luke 17:5, 6 for Jesus' explanation of faith as seed, and how it grows and increases when used.)

Jesus himself said it. "Give, and it shall be given unto you . . . ."

Giving as SEED-FAITH is the second key principle of your Blessing-Pact Covenant with God.

SEED-FAITH is giving that you may receive. In doing this you give BEFORE you have received, not after.

HOW MUCH SHOULD I GIVE?

If it is a gift of time, it is seed-time. If it is a gift of love, it is seed-love. If it is a gift of money, it is seed-money. It doesn't have to be a large amount at first — but it will grow. Give of what you have and give it FIRST.

At a freshman orientation meeting I addressed at Oral Roberts University, a girl rushed up and said, "Oh, President Roberts, since coming on campus everything is in such a rush that I just don't have any time."

I said, "Have you thought of giving some seed-time to God?"

She replied, "Oh, I'm so busy going to class and getting oriented to everything that I have no time to give."

I answered, "Don't you have 15 minutes out of the whole day you could give?"

She said, "Well, I guess so. But how do I give it?"

I said, "How about giving it to some other freshman who is frantic also? Or go to a professor and ask him to give you something to do to help him with his class. Or go to the chaplain and offer him 15 minutes to help prepare to serve the spiritual needs of the students. Or why not select anybody you see who's having difficulty. Say a good word, give him a smile, offer a little prayer."

Still not understanding, she said, "But how will this help me with my time?"

I said, "First, remember God is THE Source of all your time. Next, give these few minutes each day as seed for God to multiply back in more time for you. He will renew your time constantly."

Young people catch on quickly. I saw she was getting it. I said, "It's SEED-FAITH for a miracle. From where you are this second it would take a miracle for you to have enough time, wouldn't it?"

She said, "It certainly would."

I said, "Now don't go off to your room and pray for God to give you more time. Just give Him some seed-time, and

Remember, only what you give can God multiply back. If you give nothing, and even if God were to multiply it, it would still be nothing!

then expect your miracle. This is SEED-FAITH for God to multiply back what you need most — time. So expect it to happen after you've planted the seed."

The following week I visited the Prayer Tower. There she was holding down a part-time campus job as a tour guide. She cried, "President Roberts, I've got good news! I did what you said and now the Lord is giving me all the time I need. See, I'm not rushed anymore. I've attended every class, made every assignment, and find time to work here in the Prayer Tower several hours a week. It's a miracle!"

I have had opportunity to share the thought of seed-time with many people. I have never seen it fail when it becomes SEED-FAITH.

Remember, only what you give can God multiply back. If you give nothing, and even if God were to multiply it, it would still be nothing!

Luke 6:38 teaches us that we should make our giving of money as seed. Seed-money is thanking God in advance. It is like the grace you say before meals. You are giving thanks BEFORE the object of your thanks has been received into your mouth — as if it already had been received. It is an act of seed-planting, an act of faith of expecting a return just as the farmer does at harvesttime.

SEED-GIVING IS DIFFERENT FROM TITHING

This is why seed-giving is different from tithing. Remember, in tithing you give one-tenth AFTER you have made the income. In seed-giving, emphasized by Jesus in the New Testament, you give BEFORE the expected return.

It is both a sowing and reaping. The farmer, Jesus tells us, does it all the time. He always gives the seed to the ground first.

In seed-money you give to claim the return Jesus promised. You sow the gift for the God of the harvest to multiply back to help others, and then yourself. <u>Your continual giving is a continual renewing of your finances.</u>

I discovered this principle through a study of Jesus. I discovered the secret behind all He did in the world. It was through the life-style of giving.

He began everything He attempted with giving first. He connected giving with seed and laid down the example as the Christian's life-style. I was forced to change my thinking. Before this I had given <u>after</u> I received. But I redirected my principle of giving <u>from a debt owed, to a seed I sowed</u>. It was revolutionary but entirely scriptural. It is really the other part of tithing, the part to which people need to pay more attention.

In Malachi 3:10 and 11 God says, "Bring ye all the tithes into the storehouse, that there may be meat in mine house, and prove me now herewith, saith the Lord of hosts, if I will not open you the windows of heaven, and pour you out a blessing, that there shall not be room enough to receive it. And I will rebuke the devourer for your sakes, and he shall not destroy the fruits of your ground; neither shall your vine cast her fruit before the time in the field, saith the Lord of hosts."

It is God's promise to the tither to pour out blessings upon him, to cause material things to be renewed, and to block negative financial results.

Those who advocate tithing don't stress the law of return enough. They talk about it as a debt you owe. This is why so many give in a perfunctory way, often without any joy. They don't see that the other side of tithing is what God does in return.

Jesus went far beyond giving as a debt. Referring to tithing only one time, He said, "These ought ye to have done . . . ." (Matthew 23:23). He explained giving as the other side of tithing to be a seed sowed for God to multiply it, first, to help others, and then to help you, the giver, to receive "good measure, pressed down, and shaken together, and running over . . ." He shows His personal concern for you at the point of your need.

You see, in His concern for you, Jesus wants to show you how your SEED-GIVING makes possible two very necessary things: (1) that there may be "meat in His house," or enough to carry on His great work today, and (2) that He can take what you give and multiply back that there may be "meat in your house," or enough for your personal needs today. (See 1 Kings 17:8-16 for an illustration of this principle concerning a woman and her needs being met.)

THE THIRD KEY PRINCIPLE: EXPECT A MIRACLE!

First, turn your life over to God and look directly to Him as THE Source of your supply.

Second, because you love God and trust in Him as your Source, you give to Him FIRST. Your giving becomes seed for Him to help others, and to multiply back in the form of your need. Giving becomes your LIFE-STYLE as it was Jesus'.

God as your Source, and always giving to Him first, becomes SEED-FAITH. It is on the basis of SEED-FAITH that you have evidence to put into practice the third key principle. You expect a miracle.

I have been given the privilege of praying for a great many people with the laying on of hands. In nearly 23 years of praying for individuals and masses of people, I find that many want a prayer and a touch that will in one single instant wipe out their entire past, take care of their future, and solve all their problems in the NOW. They simply don't know the Word of God and the teaching of Jesus on SEED-FAITH, that each person must do something FIRST. You must have evidence for your faith.

For example, you wouldn't think of sitting on a chair without some evidence that it would support your weight. You have faith to sit on it only when you know the facts warrant it.

You wouldn't ride in an elevator unless you had evidence it wouldn't fall. Nor would you eat dinner tonight without knowing the food is all right.

This is how faith works. The Bible says, "Now faith is the substance of things hoped for, the evidence of things not seen" (Hebrews 11:1). Evidence. You have to base your faith on evidence; in this case, the evidence that God makes available through His Holy Word.

The great success the Blessing-Pact Covenant is having is with those individuals who come into a knowing with their faith. God is the Source to whom they look and in whom they trust. I and others are means and instruments, not sources. They give as seed, giving of their resources, their inner selves. They do this first. In their hearts they know they are doing it. And they do it from the heart. The Holy Spirit then supernaturally empties them of doubt and brings them into a state of knowing that God will do it!

HOW TO RELEASE YOUR FAITH TO EXPECT A MIRACLE

At a partner's meeting a beloved friend told me of the illness of his wife. Momentarily he was crushed. Doctors had helped but only a miracle could raise her up.

My heart went out to him. First, however, something had to be done in him. I couldn't tell him to look to God as his Source, he was already doing that. The doctors, the Christians he called upon to pray, his own prayers were means to him, not a source. I couldn't suggest he start giving, for giving is his life-style. I know of no more generous human being and child of God.

The Holy Spirit prompted me to say, "My Brother, you have given too much seed not to expect a return. Now just start expecting. God is already multiplying back your love, your compassion, your faith, your financial gifts — in fact, He is multiplying your entire spirit of giving. You have evidence for the releasing of your faith. And I'm going to expect that miracle with you."

I prayed for him and through him for his wife.. I felt a release in my spirit. The following day he brought her to the meeting. When I touched her and prayed, I stopped and said, "Something already has started happening in you, hasn't it?"

She smiled and said, "Yes."

God has told us to do certain things first as evidence to help us release our faith. When we do them, and know in our heart that we have, we come into a state of knowing.

It is while you are in this state of knowing that you can really release your faith and truly expect a miracle!

Now expecting a miracle is absolutely essential. Just as you look TO God for your supply, and give TO God as seed, so you expect a miracle FROM God.

Right here is the key point. So many have told me, "Oral Roberts, I didn't know I was to expect a miracle."

Some have said, "I didn't know I could."

A young man said to me, "I'm all straightened out on my Blessing-Pact now. There's just one thing I don't understand. Why am I supposed to expect anything?"

I laughed. "Young man," I said, "suppose a farmer plants his seed, continues to cultivate the soil and says, 'Well, I don't understand why I should expect the seed I sowed to be multiplied into a harvest. If it does, maybe it will leap up from the ground on its own, fly over and tell me it's here!' "

The boy laughed. He said, "I see that but . . ."

I said, "Why would a farmer sow seed if he didn't expect the miracle of a harvest? Every farmer I know goes to the field every day to see how much the seed has multiplied, how soon he is to send his trucks to gather in the harvest. If he didn't expect a return, likely he wouldn't check the fields. The harvest could be there and he wouldn't know it. Thus it would be wasted."

Then I gave him a Scripture, Hebrews 6:14, "Surely blessing I will bless thee, and multiplying I will multiply thee."

Listen. When you do your part and release your faith, God will send the miracle. This is why you must expect it, so you will recognize it when God sends it and reach forth and receive it from His hand. Otherwise, it may pass you by.

HOW I LEARNED TO EXPECT A MIRACLE

I was in Miami, Fla., in a crusade when I discovered this third key principle: Expect a Miracle.

My life had been threatened by an atheist who vowed he would destroy Christianity in America. I was one of his key targets. Guards were placed around me when I preached. One was near the motel where I slept.

One night I was awakened with these words from Jesus: EXPECT A MIRACLE. TELL YOUR PARTNERS TO EX-PECT A MIRACLE. TELL PEOPLE THEY CAN HAVE A NEW MIRACLE EVERY DAY.

We completed the crusade without further incident and I flew home to Tulsa. I sat down and related to Evelyn about expecting a miracle. When I finished she said, "Oral, take pen and paper and write it down exactly as you told it to me. Don't change a word. Send it to the printers and offer it as a gift to our partners."

This is how the amazing little book titled, "EXPECT A MIRACLE," was written. The first week after I offered it, more than 100,000 requests came in for it. Since then it has gone into many printings and is still one of the most sought-after little books I've written. Expect a miracle. Jesus said, "Ask, and it shall be given you; seek, and ye shall find; knock, and it shall be opened unto you" (Luke 11:9).

Paul said it: "I have planted, Apollos watered; but God gave the increase" (1 Corinthians 3:6). God gave the IN-CREASE! The increase or the miracle is there. Expect it so you will recognize it when God sends it. It will come to you in the form of your need.

This makes you look forward to every new day as the most important day in your life. Why? Because you know God is your Source. Like Jesus, giving is becoming your life-style. Therefore, you can expect a miracle — in the form of your need — every day. This creates a joy and a challenge in your new way of giving as a way of life.

I saw someone give two little boys some candy. The older was given more than the younger. When the older boy ate all he could hold, he threw the rest away instead of sharing it with the younger boy. When I saw this, it reminded me of the way most of us are and the way God sees us.

SEED-FAITH is giving and receiving; not receiving and giving. It is not (like the older boy) receiving and after consuming all one can, throwing the rest away on things that don't count in life.

A missionary was following his guide through thick jungle on his way to a new tribe. Time and again they had to take their axes and literally cut their way through the thick mass of growth.

Finally they came to an area where the growth was so thick that the sun was blotted out over them and they were in near darkness. The missionary cried, "How are we going to find our way?"

Calmly, the guide replied, "Sir, I am your way."

If you ever find a full solution to your problems and needs, it will be because you see that God is your Way, your Source, and you finally turn to Him. So why waste precious time, talent, and money seeking it through other sources?

3

HOW SEED-GIVING CAN GIVE YOU CONTROL OVER INSURMOUNTABLE PROBLEMS AND HELP YOU SOLVE THEM

BEFORE YOU READ this chapter, take your Bible and read Luke 5:1-11 for a background. Read it carefully. This is very important to you.

Peter's boat was his seed-giving. He gave it first to Jesus who used it for the preaching of the gospel. Then Jesus gave it back, saying, "Launch out into the deep and let down your net for a catch." He was saying, "I intend to multiply your giving by filling this empty boat with a record catch of fish. Just launch out into the deep, throw over your nets, and I will do the rest."

Now Peter was a commercial fisherman; he fished for a living and to support his family. He understood Jesus' language about the deep, he knew that's where the biggest fish were.

What Peter did not know was the principle of giving as seed-giving, that seed-giving is the only thing God can multiply back to you.

Peter knew about tithing. All good Jews tithed. They gave an exact 10 percent of what they had earned to God. The tithe is, in effect, a payment due, a thanks-giving of 10 percent AFTER the income is made. Peter doubtless was a tither and knew that the tithe was the 10 percent he owed.

Still he had missed the benefits of seed-giving. His boat was empty, his nets worn; he and his partners were discouraged. He said to Jesus, "We have toiled all the night and taken nothing."

A hard worker? Yes. A tither? Doubtlessly, yes. A man with a financial need? Yes. A man occupied with the futility of his own efforts? Yes.

Peter had not yet realized that Jesus was the Son of God and was introducing a new way of life for the people of God. He had come to fulfill the Law of Moses in the Old Testament and to give His blood in a New Testament, or a new covenant, that a man might have life and have it abundantly. (John 10:10.)

He brought an entirely different way of giving which, if a man would freely enter into it, would be given to him "GOOD MEASURE, PRESSED DOWN, AND SHAKEN TOGETHER, AND RUNNING OVER" (Luke 6:38).

This is summed up in Hebrews 6:14, "Surely blessing I will bless thee, and multiplying I will multiply thee."

When Jesus asked Peter to give his boat, He knew it was empty and the nets were worn. He knew business was bad and the family was in need. He knew the discouragement of toiling all night with no results. He knew something else, too. He knew that He had come in the most personal way to enter into a person's life, to be where he is, to feel his needs and sufferings. He knew that the very purpose of His atonement was that He and man might become one, a relationship so close they would be closer together than their breath or skin.

THAT YOU MAY HAVE

Jesus said, "I am come that ye may have . . ."

How different this is from what a person ordinarily asso-

ciates with coming from God. Written into building con-
tracts are such clauses as: not responsible for acts of God
such as fire, earthquakes, storms, etc.

A man horribly misshapen, desperately poor, said, "Look,
this is what God did to me."

When disaster strikes, people are hurt or killed, there are
those who say, "This is the will of God."

Not so with Jesus. "I am come," He declared, "that ye
might have life and that ye might have it more abundantly."

When His own disciples wanted to incite a riot and have
a certain city burned to the ground, He replied, "The Son of
Man is not come to destroy men's lives, but to save them"
(Luke 9:56).

The Bible says, "Every good gift and every perfect gift
is from above, and cometh down from the Father of lights,
with whom is no variableness, neither shadow of turning"
(James 1:17).

And to the children of God, "Beloved, I wish above all
things that thou mayest prosper and be in health, even as
thy soul prospereth" (3 John 2).

The father of the prodigal son said to the elder brother,
who was mad because he had received the wayward brother
back and given him new clothes and a feast with his friends,
"Son, all that I have is yours." The elder brother didn't really
know his own father. He had to be reminded that all his
father possessed was his at any time he asked for it. (Luke
15:31.)

The Bible says, "My God shall supply all your need according to his riches in glory by Christ Jesus" (Philippians
4:19).

Jesus demonstrated abundant life to all He met. He
thought in terms of their needs being met, their sicknesses
being healed, things they had been denied being restored to

them, torments they had brought on themselves being relieved, and the curse of sin over them being removed. He came in the form of their needs.

But in getting ready to bless them or to multiply His blessings back to them, He always asked them to do something FIRST.

JESUS KNEW PETER'S BOAT WAS EMPTY

There at the Sea of Galilee Jesus was concerned with the large crowd pressing in upon Him. He cared for them and their needs. This is why He wanted Peter's boat in the first place. It would make a mighty good pulpit from which the people could see and hear Him.

He had equal concern for Peter and his partners in the fishing business. He cared for them and their needs, too. He knew the boat was empty. That's what interested Him most. Had it been full He could not have used it to preach from. Nor could He have returned it with an increase.

Jesus looked on a need differently. Most people today see their needs and become negative. Often they say, "Why? Why has this happened to me? What have I done to deserve it?"

Jesus looks on a need in the most positive way. To Him, a need exists to be met. To Jesus, a need in your life is not something to discourage and make you negative. It is a legitimate claim you have upon His limitless resources to be met in full!

This is what God's Word says, "God shall supply all your need." Now SHALL is a strong word. In other words, the moment your need faces you, God's SHALL-SUPPLY PROMISE goes into effect.

This is something you need to know and get positive about. No need should intimidate or bully you. If Christ is first in your life, and you are giving to Him, you are in connection! You are plugged in. God is answering; you should be expecting. What a difference this makes in your attitude!

Since the revelation of the Blessing-Pact Covenant to me, I have studied it in the Bible from Genesis through Malachi in the Old Testament, and from Matthew to Revelation in the New Testament. In all the references to it throughout the Bible I have seen these three key principles. I constantly repeat them to myself, and so should you. Say:

1. God is the Source of my supply.
2. God wants to be first in my life and my giving. Whatever I give, I give it as SEED-FAITH.
3. I expect a miracle. What I give I expect God to use to help others and to multiply back to me in the form of my need.

We see these three key principles in Jesus' dealings with Peter and his friends, who were not accustomed to looking to God as their supply in the fishing business. They looked to themselves, to their knowledge and experience, to their own efforts. Although doubtless they were tithers, paying one-tenth of what they had already earned or what they owed to God, they had not understood Jesus' way of giving in the New Testament which is, "Give, and you shall receive." They had observed the law of seed-giving all around them but had never applied it to the relationship of their giving to God.

Seed-giving is sowing and reaping. The farmer who wants a crop first gives seed to the earth. The seed and the ground belong to each other. In the same way you, and your giving, and God belong together. It is in this interaction that the seed is multiplied.

The first thing Jesus did was to help them get their eyes off their problem. He did this by asking them to do something for Him, to give Him their boat for a little while to use in His work.

One day after I had spoken, a man stopped me. He blurted out a big problem in his marriage. As I began sharing some ways to sow SEED-FAITH that God could use to heal this marriage, he kept right on talking of his problem. I said, "Sir, you didn't hear a word of my message a while ago, did you? And you are not hearing me now."

He raised his head, looked at me and said, "I've got my mind on my problem."

I said, "You have to think about your problem enough to know what it is, but that's all."

As he looked at me with a question on his lips, I said, "At this point you either become part of the problem or the solution. I am talking to you about the solution. Do you want to hear it?"

He nodded and I shared the principles of SEED-FAITH with him. I said, "With these three key principles you are able to relate yourself and your need directly to Jesus who is the answer to this problem you face. You are defeated, however, as long as you keep your eyes on the problem. You must redirect your thinking. When you do, you will see the possibilities of your own SEED-FAITH for a healing of your marriage."

Jesus had the fishermen to do something *first*, to give Him something of themselves, in this instance their boat, so that they would start looking to Him as the Source of their supply. At that point He applied the third key principle, "Launch out into the deep and make your catch." He was saying, "There is a certain depth where the multiplying of your seed-giving starts. I know where this depth is. It is beyond the level of your old thoughts and practices of building your life pattern around yourselves. It is going beyond self to God, to that point where He is first in your life, where you give Him your best, then you ask Him for His best. That is where your miracle starts — at your depth."

There is a certain depth in your giving. What you give must represent you. You cannot compromise your depth, or what you give. You must give it first. When you do, it is a great moment in your life. For now Jesus is at the helm of your boat; He is in control of your life; He is directing you where the supply is.

Peter said with enthusiasm, "At your word, Lord, I will let down the net."

In our language today he is saying, "Lord, I'll do it, and I'll expect a miracle."

See them now. No longer are their eyes on the problem. They are looking to Him. The boat they have given to Him has been used to help others, now Jesus has restored it to them and is on His way to multiply it back — this time full and overflowing with fish which they will sell to meet the needs of their families.

They are expectant. They know something good is going to happen to them.

Now the command was given. "Here is your depth. Throw your net over." Jesus' voice was positive, His words electric. Eager hands threw the net; it settled into the water. Hungry fish struck it. Hands tightened. "Pull in the net," the voice of the Master spoke again.

The fishermen pulled and strained. In the net was their seed-giving, multiplied. Fish by the hundreds; big ones, little ones, all kinds, jumping, leaping. Now they haul it in. It's too full. The cords begin to break.

The men cry out, "It's too big for the boat. Look out, it's going to sink!"

Concerned now with the catch, or the harvest, they call

for other hands, other boats, and they are filled.

It was then that it dawned upon them. This man Jesus did what He had said, "Give, and it shall be given to you; good measure, pressed down, and shaken together, and running over, shall men give into your bosom."

WHAT THIS MEANS TO YOU TODAY

In reflecting on this encounter with their needs and what Jesus directed them to do, I want to point out that:

1. He asked them to go one more time, to try again, and this time look to Him as their Source, and to expect a miracle-catch. What if they had not tried that second time?

2. He told them there was a certain "depth" for them, and at that point their miracle would start. This is giving of yourself — money, talent, time, effort, love, patience, determination, faith. It is seed that you give to God as the farmer gives to the earth.

3. He told them to let down their nets for a "catch." Their minds had been on failure; Jesus' was on success. Theirs had been on catching nothing; His was on a miraculous catch. Theirs was on the limitation they faced; His was on the limitless resources of God.

4. He knew there was plenty; they were in the midst of it. All they had to do was to change inside, to open themselves up, begin giving to God, and expecting a miracle. There is no shortage of God's resources, Friend; none whatsoever. There is only a shortage in faith, in our understanding of the goodness of God. Stop doubting the power of your own faith in God. Release

your faith. God will show you plenty.

5. After they did something first, it set in motion the power that transformed them from nothing to something, from zero to everything. And it changed the direction in which they had been looking. Now they saw, not the problem, but Jesus. Humbled at His great concern for them, grateful for this tremendous act of supply for their needs, they saw what they needed most: a continual relationship with Jesus being first.
Peter expressed it, "Depart from me, Lord, for I am a sinful man." Jesus said, "Follow me, and I will make you fishers of men."

Today, a man may not use the same words as Peter did, for words have different meanings now. Today, a man says, "Lord, I've messed up my life. I don't feel worthy to call Your name. I can't even ask You to help me." Today, Jesus says, "Because you now know in your heart that you can't run your own life and have finally turned it over to Me, I will change you into the person who will be part of the answer instead of the problem. I will put you in position to get your needs met and to help many others. In this way you will know real life, for you will have it abundantly."

A YOUNG MARRIAGE THAT WAS HEALED THROUGH SEED-GIVING

Just before this book went to press I kept hearing about something happening to the marriage of a couple of students on the Oral Roberts University campus. I knew they had broken up shortly after their baby was born; two promising careers were badly injured.

The young man had been part of an ORU World Action musical team that traveled with me to Israel and different parts of Europe. His wife had been part of the World Action

Television Singers seen on our hour-long specials each quarter and the weekly half-hour programs.

Both were extremely talented, dedicated to God, loved their work, and should have had, by natural and spiritual standards, no marital problems.

Their breakup hurt everybody; themselves, the baby, their loved ones, their fellow students and us. The final divorce proceedings were only a month away. It looked hopeless.

I love the students at ORU. They are a part of me. What hits them hits me. It hurt when there was nothing I or anyone else could do as we saw the divorce decree rapidly approaching.

When I am on campus, I speak to the student body either in chapel or in a classroom; sometimes I speak to small groups or individuals at different times and places. Often, one of the students will share a problem or need and we talk about how Christ comes in the form of our needs. Then we will talk about how to develop a relationship with Him for this and other needs to be met in their lives.

However, I had found no way to help these two young people, at least that is the way it appeared. One thing I have discovered about young people. They hear a lot more than we think. They are independent and love to work things out in their own way. About the time you feel like giving up on them, they will often take a step based upon an idea you thought passed right over them.

Thirty days before the court was to grant the divorce, I was at a partners meeting. The World Action TV Singers had the day free so they came and sang for the partners. My Blessing-Pact partners love the students and responded warmly to their songs and testimonies that evening.

I had talked about the miracle of SEED-FAITH through

the Blessing-Pact Covenant with God. I pointed out that in the giving of anything to God there is always a "depth" God will bring to each one's mind. When we give at that depth, that's where the miracle of return begins.

I was surprised when this young wife walked over from where she sat with the singers and said, "Here's my depth. I want to start the Blessing-Pact Covenant with God for my life. Here's what I intend to give in the next 12 months."

"PRESIDENT ROBERTS, I HAVE A GREAT NEED"

She saw I was astonished at the depth, or the amount, she mentioned. She whispered, "President Roberts, I have a great need."

"But," I protested, "this seems to be over your head. God doesn't expect you to do more than you can." I was thinking, *God doesn't want you to act foolishly.*

She replied, "This is exactly what God impresses me to do. This is my depth."

I tell you there was a look of determination on her countenance that stopped me. I said, "All right. I hope you know what you're doing. I can see we're going to have to really pray for God to multiply this back and give you a miracle."

She smiled. "That's what I need, President Roberts, a miracle."

After the meeting I gathered all the students around me for some praying together. I still felt a twinge in my heart about this girl, but as we prayed and shared our thoughts they all said, "Just let people do what they feel in their hearts. God will supply." The faith of these young people lifted me higher than a mountain.

Now I can report a miracle that has touched the core of the being of this young wife and of her young husband; a miracle that continues to reveal itself in an ever-extending fashion. It has touched virtually the entire campus. It has done something in me, and certainly in this couple, their baby and their future.

THE STORY OF A MIRACLE

Asking my secretary to request them to meet me in the Dining Commons for lunch, I sat down to get their story. From my notes, here is what happened:

Me: You both look radiantly happy.

They: We are!

Me: Is the divorce going through?

They: Oh, no. We called it off just in time.

She: What you said about God being able to heal a marriage, it's happened to us, we've had a miracle.

Me: Is that why you took the Blessing-Pact a few weeks ago when I was so surprised and tried to talk you down on your depth or the amount of your seed-giving?

She: No, not specifically. I had been hearing from other students what the Blessing-Pact had meant in their lives. I wanted to take it, not for something specific, but for my whole life to get straightened out.

Me: What one thing about it attracted your interest?

She: Well, I heard you talking about all of life being in giving and receiving, and that it starts in our giving as SEED-FAITH. You said that God is the only true Source, not ourselves or anyone or any thing. You said if we would look to God as our Source and give, He would multiply it to help others

46

and ourselves. You said a miracle would happen then and we should be expecting it so we would be ready to receive it.

Me: Did you hear me say you have to do something first and this becomes evidence for your faith to act on?

She: Yes, I heard that too. As you were talking, I was wondering what I could give. You see, I've been getting $75 a month child support, my music scholarship at ORU, and through a part-time job, I get an extra $25 each month. This $25 I pay to my baby-sitter at the end of the month. You referred to the fisherman to whom Jesus said, "Launch out into the deep and throw over your nets." You said, there is a depth God will show each one in the Blessing-Pact and as we give according to our depth, that will be where our miracle will start. I saw that and asked God to show me my depth.

Me: You were really listening, weren't you?

She: I had to. I had to get quiet before God and start listening to God like I used to. That's when He impressed me that my depth was a specific amount during the next 12 months.

Me: And nearly shocked me out of my senses.

She: I had $25 and I knew I was to start my Blessing-Pact with it. So I came up and did it. You were surprised and told me maybe I should start smaller, but I was only doing what I felt inside. I had to do it.

Me: When I saw you had such a strong conviction about it, I thought, *Well, God must have a great plan for this girl's life.*

Me: Did you know she had taken the Blessing-Pact?

He: No, I didn't. It was 10 days before I learned about it.

Me: How did you feel about it?

WE HAD SHUT OUR HEARTS TO EACH OTHER

He: We both had been lying to ourselves. We kept trying to convince ourselves that we didn't love each other. Yet here we were on a campus where you can really come to know God and yourself. But we shut our hearts. We felt there was nothing we could do concerning our marriage and our baby.

Me: Obviously something has happened and you both feel love for each other now.

They: Oh, yes.

She: You wouldn't believe what has happened to us.

He: It's a whole new life.

She: Yes, it's a new beginning.

He: It's like a light has been turned on inside us. It's great.

Me: When did you first start feeling this?

She: When I put in seed-money that night it was a point of contact to help me release my faith. I had been all bottled up inside, my studies had become hard. I was very unhappy and I desperately wanted to know God's will for my life. I knew if I could release my faith God would start helping me.

He: You see, both of us had jumped at anything

that would justify letting the divorce go through.

She: Yes, I even read the Bible looking for a way to justify myself.

He: About three days after I learned she had taken the Blessing-Pact, it hit me: *You love her. You love the baby. You should call her and work things out.*

Me: You say it hit you?

He: Yes, I knew I should call her.

Me: That's what faith is, a knowing inside.

He: I knew it all right.

She: What really helped me most in your talk was that I saw for the first time that I wanted a source of supply for my life. I had messed it up and needed guidance from the right source. I had listened to different people and not enough to God. I had heard you say in chapel services that the only real Source is God. When I saw this, I knew I could find the answer.

He: I felt I should phone her and talk.

Me: Did she respond?

He: At first she was very cool. She told me to come on over. When I saw her, I felt she was different somehow.

She: I had finally got my life going in the right direction. God had become first in my life. I was really looking to Him.

He: When we married, our first mistake was to quit having devotions. Soon we began leaving God out. So when I finally realized that we had missed it, I knew we had to go back where we left off and start again with God.

She: The first $25 I put in my Blessing-Pact was what I got above child support. It was all I had left to live on that month. To me I saw it as SEED-FAITH and when I put it in, I knew I had put in myself. I can't tell you how good I felt, yet I had gone broke. It was my last money. I knew I had given my Blessing-Pact.

Me: Did God start multiplying it back?

She: Not at first. Somehow I got through the next three weeks which was the time I was to get another $25. When I received it there was an extra $25. I never knew why they did this except that they said they wanted me to have it. It was exactly my need for the baby-sitter and enough for my other needs.

He: It was about this time I felt something.

Me: I believe you said you didn't know she had made her Blessing-Pact?

He: That's right. Although we still went to classes, the only contact was through our baby daughter. That's when I phoned my wife.

She: I was still on my guard.

Me: Did you tell him you had made a Blessing-Pact Covenant?

She: No.

Me: You know, it seems to me God was working on both ends of the line. He dealt with your hearts. The inside of you was touching each other. You were touching the heart where

matters are settled.

She: God was my Source now. I fe
time in my life I now had *bei*
longer one to whom something
ing. I knew I had some contro
and I could change them. Gon
had been trying to tell myself.
the truth and I accepted it. (
come real to me.

He: And to me.

She: He knew nothing of the Blessing
had not tried it.

He: No, I had only heard about it.

She: When we got serious about goi
each other and renewing our r
told him that with a covenant wi
this we could make it.

Me: What about your baby?

They: For the first time she has a wh
and daddy.

Both of these young people are now m
World Action Television Singers. Each time I
have done our tapings and I need a little ex
all I have to do is look at them with the love s
faces.

What I like about the Blessing-Pact Cover
is that it is rooted in God, in seed that you pl
and in the solid feeling you gain in the inner
that He is going to give a miracle, and He will
right time.

There are no shortcuts, no easy answers.
exemptions from needs and problems. But the
works when, with simple, sincere faith in God,

HOW MY SISTER'S SEED-FAITH
SAVED MY LIFE AND HERS

ıster jewel was the first to sow SEED-FAITH in my
 for my healing. <u>She gave so much when she shared</u>
<u>vitness that God was going to heal me</u>. Yet years later
ı she and her husband, Leo, faced the most severe need
eir lives, she had difficulty in accepting the principle of
g and receiving in the Blessing-Pact and, as a result,
not expecting a miracle for her needs.

Vhen I was near death, she had said some revolutionary
gs to me and showed me I could be healed. As revolu-
ıry as her words were to me, however, mine were equally
lutionary to her. Just as God had come to me through
words there where I was and as I was, He came to her
ugh me in her desperate financial condition. "Jewel,"
id, "this problem need not continue harassing you and
. You can get it met. You can get a miracle."

'But how?" she asked.

Her need had become so big in her mind that it defied
tion. It looked bigger than God! It had brought them to
point of <u>zero</u> in their finances.

Leo was a carpenter and through tight money in the
lding industry, construction projects had shut down and
ıwn him and thousands of other men out of work. Months

52

had gone by. He and Jewel had raised a garden, done part-time jobs where available and managed to get by. Now the part-time work was shut off. With their savings used up, bills piling up, winter coming on, Jewel was half sick with worry and frustration.

Like millions of Christians, it had not entered her mind that a problem or need exists, not to torment and confuse and frustrate, but to be met by our Lord and enable us to make further progress with our lives.

She had conceived of God as the Source of my healing years before. She had freely given to inspire me to have faith that I could be healed. She was present the night I was prayed for and believed with all her heart God would raise me up by a miracle of healing. She saw me healed.

She had practiced these three key principles of the Blessing-Pact for me. Yet at her own point of need she had not thought of God as the Source for a job. She had not thought of giving her way into receiving a solution. The idea of expecting a miracle for anything like a job escaped her entirely.

This was fragmenting her life into different parts. She believed God was vitally concerned with saving the soul, and even believed in the possibility of healing as she had demonstrated with me. Mundane affairs such as employment and supply for financial needs were parts of life that were not necessarily included in God's total concern and provision. So she thought.

IN EARTH, AS IN HEAVEN

But in the prayer our Lord taught us to pray, you will see this in a different way. "Our Father which art in heaven, Hallowed be thy name . . . . Thy will be done in earth, as it is in heaven. Give us this day our daily bread." (Matthew 6:9-11).

You face all kinds of needs, including food, clothing, shelter, and a car. All this takes money. God knows this. He wants to be the Lord of your entire life, not just your soul.

This becomes a personal prayer to God our Source for His will to be done <u>in earth</u> as it is <u>in heaven</u>, and that <u>this day</u> — the now — we receive our daily bread. If we pray, as Jesus taught us, that God's will be done IN EARTH (the substance from which our bodies are made) it makes a whole lot of difference. It affects us where we are, and as we are, as God intended.

I don't think I have ever seen Jewel so hopeless as she was when she came to our house and poured out her heart. Fiercely independent, she wouldn't accept outside help. But she could talk to her brother. We had always been close.

Until that time I had not offered the Blessing-Pact to a relative. But it was the only thing I could offer her that would really work and I made the plunge.

"God is your Source, Jewel," I said.

She replied, "If only the construction business would start up again, Leo could return to work and everything would be all right."

I said, "Leo's employment doesn't depend on that."

Startled, she said, "Well, it certainly does. He's a carpenter, you know."

"Yes, I know that," I answered. "And God is in the business of supplying the needs of His children, too. Maybe this need came to teach you something about the Lord you've never thought about before."

She said, "What do you mean?"

I said, "God as Source controls all the <u>means</u> of employment. He is not dependent on any one <u>means</u>. He even controls the unexpected sources."

DON'T DIVIDE THE SPIRITUAL AND PHYSICAL

As she listened, this is the gist of what I shared with her: "Right now you have divided God's concern between the spiritual and physical. Going to church all these years and listening to all the sermons, you have missed this. Jewel, God loves you. He is concerned with you as a person. As a person you face all kinds of needs including food, clothing, shelter, a car, and other things you need in the earth. All this takes money. God knows this. He wants to be the Lord of your entire life, not just your soul."

How she listened when I said that. "I want you to do three things and get this need met," I said. "FIRST, put your mind directly on God to open up a source even though the construction business is in a slump. SECOND, start giving to the Lord and when you give, make it SEED-FAITH for God to multiply it. Remember, Jesus says that receiving follows giving. Then, THIRD, start expecting a miracle."

She said, "Oh, Oral, when I give I don't expect anything back."

"Well, what do you do when you give?"

She replied, "I just give, that's all."

I said, "When you give, who are you giving to?"

She answered, "To the Lord."

"In other words," I said, "even though you give to the church, or to some person, you are really giving to God? Is that right?"

"Yes, that's right."

"Fine," I said. "Your giving is to God. In the same way, look to God as the Source of your supply, not those who are the recipients of your giving. God is the One you have in mind. When you give, God is the One you are giving to, so start looking to Him as the One who will take what you give to help others, and multiply it back to meet your needs."

THE FARMER SOWS FOR A HARVEST

As she was trying to comprehend this, I said, "It's just

like a farmer, Jewel. Do you think a farmer sows seed in his ground and doesn't expect it to be multiplied back in a harvest he can use as a medium of exchange to secure the things he needs? Or, do you think that after sowing his ground, he doesn't expect his ground to be his source of supply but looks somewhere else? No. The ground is his source. The seed is his giving. And then he expects the miracle of harvest. At harvesttime he's out there reaping and gathering in the abundance for which he sowed seed first."

She said, "But I've never been taught that I'm supposed to receive anything back."

I said, "We were reared the same way, but God showed me differently. Whatever you give — money, talent, time, love — it's really a part of yourself you are giving. It's seed. Give, and you shall receive is what our Savior tells us. To receive, you have to expect. If you don't expect, how will you know God has sent the miracle? But when God sends it — and He will — and you are looking for it, you will be watching and will recognize it and gladly receive it for your needs."

Jewel said, "Oral, we've been out of work so long we don't have anything to give."

I said, "Do you believe what I am sharing with you is real and from the Lord?"

She said, "I do now."

I replied, "Do you believe that if you make a Blessing-Pact Covenant with the Lord and practice these three principles as SEED-FAITH, God can give Leo a job?"

"Yes, I believe God can do anything," she said.

"And give you a job, too?"

"Yes."

"Do you have anything left to give as seed-money?"

"Well, I have $2, that's every cent I have left."

"Give it as your best to the Lord, then ask Him for His best. The greater the sacrifice, the greater the blessing."

She said, "I'll start my Blessing-Pact with my last $2."

I answered, "Jewel, you've sowed a lot of seed to the Lord in your life. You sowed SEED-FAITH to help me get my healing. Don't think that God doesn't see all this. Now you've begun to see that through your giving you can re-direct your faith. You can know that it is actually seed for an expected harvest; you can have a solid basis on which to use your faith. And remember one other thing: each time you give, make it a point of contact to help you release your faith to God to receive this miracle."

I felt good about it and she did, too. I could almost see her inner woman standing up inside, the depression slipping away from her heart, the hopelessness leaving. When she left she said, "Oral, I've always believed in your ministry. I know God talks to you. Maybe I don't understand all you told me about the Blessing-Pact Covenant, but I trust you and I believe it will work."

"It will, Jewel," I said. "It will."

JEWEL BECAME A NEW PERSON

Nothing I do gives me such joy as when I share these principles with the people who are faced with needs. These principles are eternal and they will never fail.

About two or three weeks later there was a knock on our front door. Evelyn said, "Oral, it's Jewel."

One look at her and I knew God had answered. "Tell me about it," I said. I thought she would burst as she said, "A contractor called Leo and said he had a job for him for five months, and the way things look it will be permanent work. The wages are good."

"What else?" I asked.

"You know," she said. "You know."

Yes, I knew. I had heard she had obtained a job, also.

She said, "And it's the best job I've ever had. I work with wonderful and congenial people. There's no smoking or drinking or cursing or fighting among the company and the people. It's what I've always wanted. Oral, it really works, doesn't it?"

The story of Jewel and Leo was carried in the October 1969 issue of ABUNDANT LIFE Magazine. There they testified to continuous employment over these 10 years. They own their home, are ardent workers in God's kingdom, and are hopeful people. They have had other needs and will have new ones in the future. But as Jewel said when interviewed recently by a reporter, "I look on our needs in a different way. I understand the Blessing-Pact. Every need is there to be met. I know God will do it, if I do something first."

5 HOW I LEARNED A LESSON EARLY IN MY MINISTRY TO LOOK TO GOD AS MY SOURCE FOR A LOAN

EARLY IN THIS MINISTRY I was answering my mail in our dining room. The mail kept increasing until we had to take over the garage. Then the entire house.

We moved to another house and settled down, not dreaming the mail would continue to increase until an office would have to be secured.

Soon I was looking for a larger building to rent. When nothing suitable was available I had the feeling that God wanted us to build one. My problem was this: I had no money to construct the building. I realized loans would have to be obtained. But how?

First I saw a piece of ground that impressed me. As I stepped it off, something seemed to say, "This is your lot." The price was reasonable, but I didn't have the full purchase price and they would sell for cash only.

A man who had been blessed through the Blessing-Pact principle came to my mind. I called him and told him about the ministry's growth and the urgent need for larger quarters to serve the people. He asked me the price of the lot. I told him. He said, "How much do you need?"

I said, "I have half of it; I need the other half which I can repay over a period of time."

He said, "I'll pray about it."

In the mail came his check for the whole amount. I called him back. "You made a mistake. I only need half this amount."

He said, "You can use it, can't you?"

I said, "Yes, I can apply it toward the construction."

He said, "Just give me your word that you'll pay it back over a certain period of time."

I did. Then I woke up to the fact that a miracle had happened.

People don't lend money on land, only on the improvements. I hadn't asked this man for the entire loan. I only needed one-half the purchase price of the lot. He sent the full price.

In those days the Blessing-Pact principle was just coming into my thinking. I allowed the ease with which the purchase money for the lot had come to give me a false confidence.

With the deed to the lot in hand I paid a visit to the bank where I had secured my first small loan. I had paid this back on time and had a good relationship with the bank.

COME BACK IN FIVE YEARS

To my surprise, when I applied for a building loan the banker said, "Come back in about five years after you've had experience and we'll let you have the money."

I couldn't understand it. I went back a second time and got another refusal. I knew no one else in the whole world to whom I could turn. Naturally, I had turned to the ones I knew; the first helped me, the other one had refused.

For days I prayed and meditated over this. Gradually I began to learn things. I discovered I no longer liked this banker. His refusal had canceled from my mind the appre-

God didn't say He would supply my needs with His riches in heaven, but according to His riches in heaven by Christ Jesus. That means here in the now. (Read Philippians 4:19.)

ciation of his first loan to me. I asked myself, "Why did he make the first loan? I was not nearly as good a financial risk then as I am now."

The banker had said, "Mr. Roberts, you are a sincere young man. We believe you are doing a good work. But you are in religious work. Therefore, from a business standpoint we have no guarantee you can repay the bank."

I said, "I paid off the first loan."

He said, "Yes, your record is good so far. But what if you died? What if the people stop supporting your work? You are asking for several thousand dollars. It's too risky for the bank. Now after you have operated for five years, you will have established yourself and . . ."

That's when I left.

One day while in prayer, I was asking God to make this banker open up to us. As I did, I felt a check in my spirit. I remembered Philippians 4:19, "But my God shall supply all your need according to his riches in glory by Christ Jesus."

GOD IS MY SOURCE

I thought, *This banker is not God. He doesn't control all the money I need; God does. However, God's riches are in heaven and that's a mighty long way off.* That's when it hit me. God didn't say He would supply my needs with His riches in heaven BUT ACCORDING TO HIS RICHES IN HEAVEN BY CHRIST JESUS. God was telling me that He is not poor. He was saying that it's all on deposit in heaven but payable in the coin of the realm down here IF I WOULD LOOK TO HIM AS MY SOURCE.

I never felt better in my life. With God as THE Source, and with my needs being supplied according to the amount of riches there is in heaven, I would find the loan; the building would be constructed, and I would be able to serve the people.

My inner man was now standing up instead of lying down. When I thought of the banker, I no longer disliked him, for he was only doing his job according to standard banking rules. I even prayed for God to bless him for the first loan he had made to help me get started. Then I found myself praying for God to supply this loan I needed.

I had discovered a principle that was to serve me in the future when many other loans, all of them larger, would be needed. I had discovered the one infallible Source: God is the Source of supply for all my needs. There would be times when I would forget this principle or neglect to apply it, but ultimately I would stake all my future supply on it and it would never let me down.

Evelyn knew something had happened to me. The brooding I had been going around with was gone. She said, "Honey, you must have gotten the loan."

I said, "No, but I will soon."

She said, "From the bank?"

I said, "Apparently not, but it's coming."

She said, "From where?"

I said, "From God."

Then I explained the new understanding I had found in God's Word. I said, "If our banker doesn't help us, God has somebody who will."

I dismissed the banker from my mind. However, it was not long until he found himself changing his mind. Men who run lending institutions may think they are in control, but when they are dealing with a man who has begun to look to God as THE Source of his supply, they find that God will move heaven and earth, if necessary, to meet his needs.

A NEW FRIEND CROSSES MY PATH

Meanwhile a man had flown to one of our crusades to

observe. While there he saw the largest number of people converted in a single service he had ever seen. He saw some miracles that astonished him. One was a boy who had stammered all his life and after the healing prayer he could speak perfectly. Another was an alcoholic who was freed and restored to his family. A third was a Commander in the United States Navy who had entered the prayer line for the healing of an incurable illness. He had returned at the end of the crusade to tell how the Navy doctors had X-rayed him and pronounced him totally free from the disease.

The man who had flown to the meeting observed all this. He talked with several of the people who had been helped. Then he met me. His name was Lee Braxton, a banker and mayor in his city in North Carolina.

At our next crusade he was present with his family. He was also at the following crusade. Finally, he flew to Tulsa to investigate our standing in our home city. He talked to people we did business with, the newspapers, and many others. He liked what he heard and saw.

Then he came to the house where we were struggling to answer our mail. He saw me laying out the proof pages of our monthly magazine on the floor. There was literally no room elsewhere in the house.

He said, "Oral, this ministry has in it the seed of a worldwide spiritual renewal. It's going to grow and touch millions of lives. You've got to build an office and do this work in a businesslike way instead of piecemeal like you're having to do here."

I knew very little about business but I understood that what he said was right. I told him of the refusal of the bank and that I didn't know any other place to go. I said, "However, since the bank's refusal I have come into a new understanding of God's supplying our needs. God is going to work it out for the office to be built."

This knowledge had been revealed to me through God's Word as I studied it and I knew it couldn't fail. Outwardly, nothing was changed. But the inside of me was different. I had a knowing inside that God was in the center of my thoughts concerning this need for an office.

Some people think you're crazy or something when you talk like this. For them everything must fit into their own little plan and reasoning. If it doesn't, they are apt to go to pieces or get bitter and resentful. Sometimes they end up saying, "Why has God let this happen to me?"

Maybe God lets this happen to us to show us who our Source of supply really is, and how futile our own way is.

By this time, Lee Braxton himself had been helped through this ministry. He had received a healing, also his son had been healed. In addition, Lee's faith had been increased to the possibility of greater miracles in his life. He was an experienced businessman; I had asked scores of questions and he had answered them. We were now on familiar terms.

Lee said, "Oral, what are you going to do about your new office?" I replied, "Leave it to God." Now I had my thoughts on Him.

I COUNTED MY ASSETS

He said, "Why don't you go back to your banker, and let me go with you this time."

I said, "Fine, but he's already told me I don't have enough assets or experience."

Lee said, "Come on, I'll go with you."

As we went I counted up my assets:

I knew God was at the center of my life.
I knew God is a good God.
I had demonstrated that God answers prayer

and even performs miracles of healing.

I believed in what I was doing.

I had been giving generously to God's work.

I had SEED-FAITH working.

People were getting help and their number was increasing every month.

I was sincere, honest, a hard worker, and had faith.

I was expecting help from God and knew it would come sooner or later.

Those assets looked and felt mighty good to me. They were evidence on which I could release my faith.

The banker, I knew, was impressed with me as a person, as a man who paid his bills, as one interested in helping people. These were assets but not the kind the bank examiners would look at if they saw a big loan on the books of his institution.

My work had been incorporated as a nonprofit organization. Its financial assets were few. Its future was bright. From a cold, logical point of view, this was not enough. But God, I knew, was enough.

When we entered the bank Lee said, "Wait a minute, Oral. Here's what I want you to tell the banker: Tell him that Lee Braxton is president of the First National Bank in his city back in North Carolina; he's been here, likes what he sees, and his bank will lend you the money you need to construct the new office."

I replied, "But, Lee, if your bank is going to do that why should I even see this banker?"

Lee said, "Just do as I tell you."

We went into the office of the president. I introduced Lee and blurted out what Lee had told me to say.

The president turned to Lee and said, "Mr. Braxton, you

tell your bank to keep its money in North Carolina. We'll take care of our friend, Oral Roberts, here."

THE SOURCE THAT NEVER FAILS

You could have knocked me over with a feather. I didn't have any faith that this man would change his mind. Yet suddenly I had a loan of several thousand dollars from the same bank that had refused me twice before. I was the same man, my assets hadn't changed, still I was looking at a miracle. I realized I was looking at something else too — the Source that never fails: God.

"Thank you very much," I said. "I'll accept the loan." The papers were signed and in less than an hour we were on our way home.

When I returned a few weeks later to get the first installment on the loan, the president smiled and said, "Reverend Roberts, I should have my head examined. I just don't know what possessed me to make this loan."

I smiled right back and said, "I know."

"Yes, I guess you do," the banker replied.

This incident in my life was large at the time. It has helped me in much larger ones since, for through the growth of this ministry I've been forced to become, not only an evangelist, but a businessman.

Paul had to learn to be a businessman, too, as well as being called of God to preach the gospel. He carried his business with him — tentmaking. I know he faced many of the same problems I have had to face. But he found God was sufficient in the same way I have come to see Him. It was Paul who said, "But my God shall supply all your need according to his riches in glory by Christ Jesus" (Philippians 4:19). Paul had tested this mighty Source and found it never-failing.

6

A CONVERSATION WITH JEWISH FRIENDS CONCERNING SEED-FAITH

RECENTLY I VISITED with a dear Jewish friend of mine. He and his family were at a Tulsa restaurant and he invited Evelyn and me to sit with them. He was telling me how he enjoyed our telecasts, particularly the way I talked about God being in the now. Then he told me this story:

He: You know, of course, the difficulty I've had with a certain piece of land we have. I have been working virtually day and night on it for the past six months — trips to Los Angeles, trips to Washington, D. C., and trips to New York. Also, I have had conferences with our city officials and my bankers. Frankly, I've not been too successful in my efforts. Reverend Oral (this is what he always calls me), I received your plaque, "Something GOOD is going to happen to you." I placed it where my staff and I could see it. It has been fascinating to see the change in all of us, including my personal secretary.

Me: What kind of change?

He: It perked us up. For the last three days I have had a feeling come over me that I can't describe. Each night as I went to bed I said my prayers. In my prayers I repeated some of the things I heard you say on television.

Me: What's that?

He: I said, "Lord, Reverend Oral says You are concerned with our concerns. Reverend Oral comes to You through Jesus. I don't know much about Jesus so I am coming in the best way I know — directly to You. Reverend Oral has been praying for me through Jesus. Hear both our prayers, Lord." The sweetest feeling has come over me. I am not saying that I have come as close to God as I desire but I feel differently.

Me: Thank God. I know that feeling.

He: Yesterday morning I went to my two banks. The men I deal with there are not always too friendly, though sometimes they are. This time I went in and I knew something good was happening to me, especially inside me. The banker looked up, saw me and said, "Well, what's come over you?" I said, "Something good is going to happen to me." He replied, "I know who you've been talking to." I said, "My good friend, Reverend Oral Roberts." He said, "Yes, I know. He sent me one of those plaques too. It's terrific." Then he said, "What can I do for you today?" I told him the amount I needed. He smiled and said, "You've got it." I went to my next bank and the same thing happened there. The banker said, "We'll take care of you." I thanked him and left. I always figure when they say, "Yes," that it is time to leave.

Me: I know that this project of yours is worthy. God will continue helping you.

He: I feel it. Something good is coming.

Me: What you have done is to use the principle of what I call the Blessing-Pact.

He: Tell me about the Blessing-Pact.

Me: First, God is your Source. Whether the bankers go with you all the way is not too important. If you keep God as the Source of your supply, He will touch these bankers or someone else to be His instrument to help you. He is Source; men are instruments. Second, Jesus said, "Give, and it shall be given to you . . . ." If I were trying to develop this acreage, I would first give something to the Lord as seed-money for Him to multiply back. For only what I give, can He multiply to help others and to come back to me. In the Old Testament you were taught to tithe. You give 10 percent of what you have already received. This is what you owe to God. Isn't that right?

He: Yes, that's right.

Me: Jesus fulfilled the Old Testament by giving us a New Testament or New Covenant. It is a higher law. In this higher law Jesus goes far beyond the tithe. He takes it out of the area of a debt we owe and elevates it to the area of sowing a seed that we may receive — or sowing seed for a harvest.

He: Please explain further. This is very interesting to me.

Me: I have always tithed, too, but sometimes without any joy. Jesus teaches that it is more blessed to give than to receive; that as we give, it shall be given back to us good measure, pressed down, and shaken together, and running over, shall men give to our bosom; for with what measure we give it shall be measured back to us.

He: Beautiful.

Me: I used to wonder what Jesus meant by saying that it's more blessed to give than to receive. Now I know.

He: Tell me.

Me: Well, according to Jesus, what you give, whether it's love or faith or money or anything else, it is SEED-FAITH. All of life is in the seed. You are a product of seed. So am I. Even Jesus is called the Seed of David. Jesus talked about an eternal law, "Whatsoever a man soweth, that shall he also reap" (Galatians 6:7). You sow seed, you reap a harvest. You give as seed, you receive it back multiplied many times. But — and this is important — if you give nothing, and it is multiplied . . . .

He: It is nothing!

Me: Exactly. The hole you give through is the hole you receive through.

His wife: Would you repeat that?

Me: The hole you give through is the hole you receive through.

His son: That's very interesting.

Me: I feel you are learning quite a bit about Jesus.

He: That's by watching you on TV as you talk about Jesus.

Me: Getting back to your project. Everything I've ever attempted, building a university, getting on national television, or important things in my personal life, Evelyn and I always give something first.

He: You mean, instead of tithing I should give as I would plant a seed?

Me: Jesus said only one thing concerning tithing: "Ye pay tithe . . . and have omitted the weightier matters of the law, judgment, mercy, and faith: these ought ye to have done, and not to leave the other undone" (Matthew 23:23). Jesus teaches that tithing is a debt you owe and it cannot be a substitute for doing right unto others. He teaches that giving is far more than money. Money is an expression of yourself. The money you get represents your time, skill, and effort. Your money is really you. You give money and it means you give what you are — something negative or something positive. Jesus wants you to give as SEED-FAITH — your love, your respect for others, your faith, your money. Then He wants you to know that this gift is seed which He will multiply back to you good measure and running over.

His son: When I give I enjoy it. I feel good all over.

Me: Just so. That's because you open yourself up to God

when you give. You know it will come back to you multiplied.

He: You said there are three things you do in the Blessing-Pact. What is the third?

Me: The third is based on the first two. You start by turning your life and thoughts to <u>God</u> as the <u>Source</u>. God is your supply, God is the hope of your whole existence. The next is to <u>give that you may receive</u>; each gift being seed for God to multiply to help others and to come back to you, as Jesus said. I have discovered in more than 20 years of this ministry that in anything I am attempting to do, <u>if I make God my Source of supply, if I cheerfully give as Jesus told me to, then I can EXPECT A MIRACLE.</u> Expecting a miracle is the third part of the Blessing-Pact.

He: You call it a miracle?

Me: Yes, I do. How can you explain the growth of a seed otherwise? Others may say it's a good result. I know it's something beyond man's power to give. It's extraordinary; it can't be explained in human terms. Man has tried to simulate a seed — only to fail. To me, it's a miracle.

He: After you have done the first two, do you always expect a miracle?

Me: Well sometimes I forget, or get busy and let it slip. But I've learned that when I put God first as the Source of my life and my supply, when I give SEED-FAITH, God always sends a miracle. If I am looking for it, when it comes I recognize it and put forth my hand and receive it. If I am not expecting, I usually miss it. But expecting a miracle every day can become a way of life and this makes every day exciting — wondering what God will do today.

She: Oh, I see that.

Me: God always tells you to do something first. So many people are waiting on God. But God has already done it.

You Jewish people know your Old Testament. God gave us the prophets and their prophecies. In the New Testament He gave us Jesus to show us what God is like; that God is concerned with our concerns; that God is in the now; that through His Son we can find and know God. Yes, God has already given, now He is waiting on us to recognize Him as our eternal Source.

He: As the Higher Power.

Me: Sure. Call Him what you will. I call Him God, the Source of my supply. God gave us Jesus, that we might have life more abundantly. Therefore, we give, and <u>when we give we put ourselves in a position to receive all that He has provided</u> for us. And <u>He has provided for our every need</u>. Now we expect a miracle. It gives you a feeling of . . . .

His son: Optimism.

Me: Yes, <u>eternal optimism</u>. You cease being negative and become positive in your whole being. You know God is going to cause something good to happen to you. If something bad happens, as it frequently does, just keep watching, a miracle will come. So, take it and be thankful to God.

She: Oh, I wish I could practice that every day.

Evelyn: All this is in Oral's book that he is now writing. I'll see that you get a copy.

(This, of course, is the book: "Miracle of SEED-FAITH.")

On the way home, Evelyn said, "Oral, I can see how this ministry is going to reveal Jesus to many Jewish people. It's sowing the seed and someday there will be a harvest."

I profoundly believe this. I said, "Not only to the Jews, but to people of every race and walk of life."

Jesus Christ is my Lord and Savior. By His shed blood my sins are forgiven and I have been made a new person. The Blessing-Pact is a principle to help get needs met in my earthly life, and to enable me to help others. It is SEED-

FAITH which I sow by always looking to God rather than some specific person or institution as the Source of supply for my needs. I give as seed-love or SEED-FAITH, or seed-money for God to multiply back. I expect a miracle and watch for it so that I may recognize and receive it. Then I am grateful to God for His blessings.

The failures I have had are not with the Blessing-Pact but by improperly applying it. In these failures I am learning to check myself with the threefold principle of the Blessing-Pact. Usually I can find at what point I got my mind off applying the principles and can begin correcting it.

There is more in the conversation I had with my Jewish friend:

He: Reverend Oral, I must tell you again how astonished I was at the wonderful reception my bankers gave me when they had not done this before.

Me: The difference is that something had happened inside you. The bankers hadn't changed. The change was in you. The good reception was unavoidable. The inside of you influenced the inside of them.

He: That's amazing.

Me: Something more amazing is that you can repeat this time after time. God is in control on this earth more than you think. He can cause men to change toward you by what has happened in your spirit. They cannot resist you if you do what God says. Call this what you will. I know it is God through His Son, Jesus. I have never seen it fail when practiced unselfishly from the heart.

He: I am going to think on this.

Me: It will work spiritually. It will work for financial needs. And it will work on any amount, small or large. God is concerned with our concerns. What we must do is get concerned with Him and what He wants us to do with our lives and ambitions and hopes.

In thinking back over this conversation with my Jewish friends, let me say this: There isn't a doubt in my mind about the Blessing-Pact principle working in anyone who will sincerely turn his life over to God. The principle will work, if you will work it. It has to be applied.

Remember, in any area of life anything that can go wrong, usually does. If you leave things to themselves, they will never be put right; they will get worse. It's like weeds. You have to cut them out and replace them with seed of your selection, seed that you plant and tend and that will produce the right harvest.

Waiting on God won't do it. God has already done His part. He has created and set in motion the principles of SEED-FAITH for you to follow in a Blessing-Pact Covenant with Him. Apply the principles with faith and you will find God is Source, God is Multiplier, God is Miracle-Worker. And it is in your life that it will come to pass.

7

HOW TWO YOUNG MEN THROUGH APPLYING THE PRINCIPLES OF SEED-FAITH BECAME TULSA'S THIRD-LARGEST BUILDERS

I KNOW TWO YOUNG MEN who started in the building business when they had borrowed only enough money to start one little house. By struggling and working virtually day and night they got a little nest egg and were able to build two and then three houses at a time.

One day they came to Oral Roberts University with a check. "We want to make an investment here," they said.

Misunderstanding their intent, one of my associates asked what they had in mind. "Oh, just as we have found we have to invest in a good building lot before we can sell the house we construct on it, we understand God expects us to give so He will have something to build on in our business, and something He can multiply back."

When I learned of this, I knew they had heard at least a little about the Blessing-Pact. One day I sat down with them. "Young men," I said, "are you giving to your church?"

"We sure are," they said.

"What caused you to get interested in ORU?"

"Well, it's just getting started, and so are we. We know God raised it up and it's going to grow. We want to grow too."

Looking at them I could see myself at their same age, not

yet quite 30, when I began to see the principle of giving as SEED-FAITH.

"This thrills me," I replied. "If you will honestly put God first in your personal lives, in your family relationships, and in this new business venture — if you will do this by looking to God as your Source, by making giving your life-style just as Jesus did, and by expecting a miracle when you've done all you can — if you will do this sincerely and with faith, God will prosper you, and it will be to His glory. You will have the favor of God."

How serious they were as they listened. One said, "We saw it working for you. We saw you start the University with not even the first dollar, just a belief in your heart. We've seen you with your back to the wall several times, when we couldn't figure any way you could win. But you did. We understand that you start everything you do with something you give."

I said, "Yes, that's right. The only projects that have ever gone over big were the ones I started by giving to the Lord first. And there's something else."

The other one said excitedly, "Tell us. Tell us."

GOD ALWAYS HAS ME TO START AT ZERO

Naturally when he was so enthusiastic, I opened my whole heart. I said, "I try to start my projects looking to God as my Source. In one way I've been forced to for there has never been any money to start with. · God always has me to start at zero and I've found if I have my mind on God, that point is not too bad at which to start. Then, as I indicated, I give. However, the really big thing I do is after I've started doing these things, I expect a miracle from the hand of God. That, my young friends, is the final nail you drive into the building; you expect God to send a miracle."

Were they excited! "Do you mean we can have miracles like that in our business? We're not ministers of the gospel, you know, we are just a couple of young Christian laymen."

I said, "What I've been sharing are the principles of the Blessing-Pact. The principles are eternal. They apply to any situation in life. They work in whoever will work them."

They asked me to lay hands on them and pray. I did. As they were leaving one said, "We'll be back." So every few weeks when they started a new building project, here they came with a check. "More SEED-FAITH, Fellows?"

"Yes, Sir, more SEED-FAITH."

I told Evelyn about them. Together we have watched them grow spiritually, in their business, and as forces for good in the Tulsa community.

One day the younger one said, "Have you heard what my partner is doing?"

"No, tell me."

"He's started a prayer group in his home one night each week. Already about seven other young builders have accepted Christ."

Another day he said, "My partner just led a television personality here in Tulsa to the Lord."

"What are you doing?" I said.

"I'm helping him."

Then a short time later, one of the most interesting things happened. They had started their biggest building project. And out they came with another check for the Lord's work first. One of them always told me something the other one had done for the Lord or what had happened to him. I knew of course that both were involved. Anyway, one said, "Did you hear about my partner's latest miracle?"

He said, "When he got up one day last week He told the Lord, 'Lord, give me my miracle today.' As he drove to our office he had his mind on the Lord and was talking to Him about his miracle."

I replied, "You mean he's come to the place where he believes God has a miracle for him each day?"

IT'S NATURAL TO EXPECT GOD TO GIVE US A MIRACLE

He said, "Well, I'll tell you. We've got so many things going now, and we're talking to the Lord so much about each one, it's just natural when we reach our limit to expect Him to give us our miracle."

I thought, *If every child of God could hear this!*

"Did his miracle come?"

"It sure did, that same day."

"How?"

"My partner sat down in the office, opened his Bible to start the day right, and said a blessing over the day, and asked God to use him and me for His glory. About this time our secretary looked in and motioned to him. A woman was there, wanting to buy one of our properties that we desperately needed to sell. She didn't look as if she could buy anything. When my partner told her the price, she just wrote out a check in full, thanked him, and said to make out the contract."

I said, "What did your partner say to this?"

"He just smiled and said, 'Thank You, Lord, for my miracle today and, Lord, I'll be expecting another one soon.'"

"This excites me," I said. "I know you are really serving God. Just keep it up. It has yet to be seen in any walk of life what God will do through someone who will really trust Him, give to Him, and expect from Him."

Now the third-largest builders in the fast-growing city of Tulsa, these two young men are coming on like young eagles for the Lord. I am deeply moved as I watch a miracle happening right before my eyes. They are steady, reliable, calm, hard workers. They don't expect something for nothing and as the Bible says, they are "full of faith and the Holy Ghost."

As I write, the words they said to me in our last meeting ring in my heart: "We've had so many miracles in our souls, in our finances, in our relationships with the people we deal with and in our witnessing that we are learning to be alert for a miracle at any time or place we happen to be — every day."

I believe with all my heart that everyone can rise to new heights of blessing and service to God and humanity if they will start at their zero point and apply the scriptural principles of SEED-FAITH and walk with the Lord as these two young partners are doing.

8
A MAN IN A BLACK GHETTO SAID, "HE'S JUST OUT FOR THE MONEY."

A FEW MONTHS AGO I was preaching in Harlem, that area of human need and desperation, when a man stood up and said, "Oral Roberts, wait a minute."

An usher started toward him but he waved him away, saying, "I want to say something."

"Reverend Roberts," he said, "this is about something in one of your ABUNDANT LIFE magazines you sent me several months ago."

While everyone in the audience listened, and I leaned against the pulpit, this is what he told us:

"I have lived in Harlem all my life. I was born here, grew up here on these crowded streets, got married here, and raised my family here.

"When a man gets married in Harlem and has a family, he faces many problems. One of them is a need for a home. You see, in Harlem a man is not counted successful unless he has his own home. These people here tonight know what I'm talking about."

The people nodded their heads. "That's right," they said.

The man continued, "Well, I never had a home. One day I was feeling depressed over this when your magazine came. I started reading one of your articles. It was on the

Blessing-Pact, where you talked about Jesus' saying, 'Give, and it shall be given unto you; good measure, pressed down, and shaken together, and running over, shall men give into your bosom' (Luke 6:38).

"GOD SHOWED ME I WAS NOT DOING MY PART"

"When I read this, it upset me so much I threw the magazine on the floor. I thought, *Always talking about money. All he wants is for me to send him some money. He's just out for the money.*

"But something came over me and told me to pick up that magazine and read it again. I did. As I read your article again, God showed me He had much for me that He had never given me because I wasn't doing my part. I wasn't giving that I might receive.

"Now, some folks here tonight know me. I am a Christian. I go to church; I do all I know to do. But God showed me differently as I read what Oral Roberts said about the Blessing-Pact.

"At that time, all I had was $5. I jumped up, found an envelope, put the $5 in it, and sent it off to Tulsa and entered into a Blessing-Pact with God.

"Three months later nothing had happened. I still didn't have my house. I began to doubt a little. But I remembered how I felt in my soul when I sent off that first $5 and began my Blessing-Pact with God. I knew God was going to help me.

"The next day a man came by. He said, 'Can I help you?'

"I said, 'Do you mean it?'

"He said, 'I sure do.'

"I told him my story and he opened his purse and counted out $700. He gave it to me. I said, 'Thank You, Lord.'

When you start giving to God, you should not begin too large. Start where your faith is.

"The next week another man came by and gave me $1,100.

"A third man came and gave me some more money.

"Two of these men I had never met before, one I had."

By this time you could have heard a pin drop. Looking around, he said, "Today is a new day for me. Today, I live in my own home here in Harlem; it cost $27,000 and it's all paid for."

Applause broke out. In a voice breaking with emotion he continued, "I almost missed it when I threw the magazine down and began getting even more negative. I thought some wrong things. Then I felt this faith moving around inside me. I still have my Blessing-Pact and I'm going to have it the rest of my life."

He abruptly sat down. Again there was applause. I finished my sermon and prayed for the people. As I was leaving he came over and shook my hand, saying, "I almost missed it and when I heard you were coming to preach in Harlem, I knew I had to come and tell you."

I thanked him. Many times since I have related his story. I have thought about what he said. I remember the courage he had to stand before that audience and make a confession and then give his witness to what God had done in his life and family.

THE GREATER THE SACRIFICE, THE GREATER THE BLESSING

As I remember him, several thoughts come to my mind. One is concerning the $5, which was all that he had. When he put it in the envelope and sent it off to Tulsa to begin a Blessing-Pact with God, I know there was One who saw him do this. It was the same One who stood in the temple in Jerusalem and saw the rich giving of their wealth into the treasury. He became excited when a widow gave her mite. The greater the sacrifice, the greater the blessing, and it happened to her. "This poor widow hath cast in more than they all," Jesus said, and it was marked in heaven before Him who multiplies back again and again.

THE BLESSING-PACT WORKS EQUALLY WELL ON ANY AMOUNT

Another thought is, the Blessing-Pact works on the smallest gift or the largest, whether it's $1 or $5, or $10 or $100, or $1,000 or $10,000, or $100,000 or $1,000,000. The Blessing-Pact works equally well on any amount, if it is given as a seed and with joy.

START WHERE YOU ARE

Still another thought: When you start giving to God you should not begin too large. Start where your faith is. This man began with $5. As Paul said, "Not because I desire a gift: but I desire fruit that may abound to your account" (Philippians 4:17).

One can reach the same goal progressively without strain or doubt. There will be a time when you can "walk on water" for a larger amount, but remember, Jesus did not walk on water all the time. It is important to you to start and to start where you are and as you are.

Some people have received Christ as their Savior the very hour that they decided to make a Blessing-Pact Covenant with God. I have seen this happen time and time again in our partners meetings.

9 THE BIG QUESTION—IS MONEY GOOD OR BAD FOR YOU?

I AM CONSTANTLY AMAZED at Christian people who seem to think money is not good. They consider it tainted — something evil, filthy lucre. And they quote Scriptures as a basis for their belief.

What they are doing of course is misquoting the Apostle Paul. He said, "The love of money is the root of all evil" (1 Timothy 6:10). He said LOVE OF MONEY (not money itself) is the root of all evil.

Paul is right. To love money for its own sake creates serious problems in your life. The most serious one is that you put money as another god before the Lord, which God warns you against in the First Commandment. (Exodus 20:3.)

From God's viewpoint, He wants you to have money. "Beloved, I wish above all things that thou mayest prosper..." (3 John 2). He does not want you to love money itself. But He wants you to have it because it is a necessary instrument to meet needs in your life that no other instrument can.

I recall a couple attending one of our lay seminars at ORU. Both had plenty of money, but neither was living a normal and happy life. She suffered with intense pain and there was no cure in medical science, despite her ability to pay for the very best. He was miserable because he felt unfulfilled in his career.

When I talked about giving, they shut off their minds before I could explain that it is seed. Instantly they thought of their money, saying, "Well, why does God want our money?"

I said, "God doesn't want just your money. He wants you. When Jesus spoke of giving that you might receive, He included money but included other important forms of giving. This includes the giving of seed-love, seed-concern, seed-time, seed-patience, SEED-FAITH, a seed-smile, in fact, giving your entire self as seed for Him to use to constantly renew and replenish your lives."

What they really wanted was a prayer that presto, like magic, would banish every pain, every frustration, every negative force from their existence, leaving them totally free from concern.

It won't work. Not in the secular realm or in the spiritual arena of life.

PAUPER DISCOVERS SEED-FAITH

A man in Seattle, Wash., who was all but a pauper, working for the lowest wages in a laundry, heard me talk about the Blessing-Pact principle of SEED-FAITH. "It starts with putting God right in the center of your life," he heard me say. "It means you start giving. You first give yourself to God. Then you start giving of your earnings, your time, your concern for others, your love and faith as seed. You give God your best, then you ask Him for His best. The greater the sacrifice, the greater the blessing. Because you put God first as the Source of all your supply, and give as seed which He will multiply back, you have evidence for your faith to really work. God as SOURCE, and God as MULTIPLIER, is the basis on which you can release your faith and expect a miracle."

In his mind, he went back over his life. It seemed that every time his imaginative mind would enable him to invent something or come up with an idea to start a business, something always went wrong.

"I began to drift," he said later, "from one job to another. When you brought your crusade to Seattle I was making a dollar an hour. I had never considered that the church or a personal God had anything to do with me or my needs. The first day, though, your preaching that God is a good God reached inside me and I found I was responding. I came forward and accepted Christ as my personal Savior. The following week I began my Blessing-Pact. You had said a man could start his Blessing-Pact Covenant with God exactly where he was in his needs — at zero if that was where he was. I not only was at zero, I was a zero."

A year passed. Each month he had been giving a certain amount to God. He had donated some of his time to help the church he had joined to build a new sanctuary. He was holding down his job. Meanwhile a quiet change was occurring inside him. In checking himself with his Blessing-Pact he said, "God had never been the Source for me. Why, I never got my thoughts any higher than my own mind. When I tried to market one of my inventions, I looked to myself. The same was true when I sought a better job. I had never given anything to the Lord. As for expecting a miracle, I felt a man created his own."

He had heard me say, "Only God is THE Source of your supply; all other sources are instruments only. When you look to Him and give to Him, do it as seed you are planting. God will return it to you either from an expected source

God as SOURCE, and God as MULTIPLIER, is the basis on which you can release your faith and expect a miracle.

or in a totally unexpected way. Don't limit yourself to the company you work for, or to the business you have, or to your own knowledge and ability. God is the Source, not anything or anyone else in the whole world. God controls all sources of supply because He himself is your supply. Therefore, after you give, expect a miracle."

HE HAD A LIVING COVENANT WITH GOD

Through his Blessing-Pact he came to believe he had a living covenant with God. As he put God first in every part of his life, he began expecting something good to happen to him (I have never seen this fail). His mind which from time to time had been creative in the mechanical field now felt a renewing of its resources. One idea that came was a hub for a four-wheel Jeep truck which would release the front drive when not needed. There was an immediate market for it since this need had not been filled by the automotive industry. Royalties started pouring in; he was able to quit his little job and engage full time in improving this hub and inventing other aids.

He fell in love with the Lord. There is no other way to say it. It was a romance of his soul with God. He increased his seed-giving to his church, to other local groups who were helping people, and he helped many individuals who had been like himself.

When Oral Roberts University was announced, he adopted it as a special part of his life, although by that time he was in his eighties. His gifts to the construction of the original buildings inspired others to give. He would always say, "The more I give, the more the Lord gives to me." He also put the University in his will to help future needy students.

When he makes a visit to the campus, he looks around

first at the buildings and says, "Just think, I had nothing and was only making enough to barely exist when I gave my heart to the Lord. The Blessing-Pact opened my eyes to my greatest opportunity to make everything I gave a seed, and to trust God to meet my needs and give me an overflow to help others." I have heard him say this several times.

He says to the students, "Don't ever think you can make it by yourself. I tried it for 70 years and it doesn't work. Take God into your life, give to Him with joy and He will do the rest. He will release you as He did me. I'll soon be gone to be with my Lord, but through Him I've had many miracles and I expect to leave some miracles behind."

Today his photograph hangs in the John D. Messick Learning Resources Center. There's a smile on his face and his eyes appear to be looking to the distant horizon. When I pass his photograph, I pause a moment to reflect upon God, the Mighty Source, the Mighty Multiplier, the Mighty Miracle-Worker.

Money to this man is not something bad and evil. The money that comes to him through the Blessing-Pact is clean money, joyous money, money that cares for and uplifts people. Because he loves God, his money loves God and people.

GOD IS CONCERNED FOR US IN THE NOW OF OUR EXISTENCE

Seeing him in 1952, when he came haltingly forward to receive Christ as his personal Savior, and seeing him recently, now ready for his Maker but with that triumphant look in his eyes, I can never thank God enough that He also cares for us <u>after</u> we are saved and <u>before</u> we go to heaven. He is concerned for us in the NOW of our existence, whether we are at zero point, or point 30, 60, or 100. He is faithful to multiply that which we lovingly give to Him of ourselves and our resources.

PART II

HOW JESUS, THE PERSON, IS THE ANSWER TO YOUR NEED

BEFORE YOU READ THIS CHAPTER, WRITE
DOWN YOUR BIGGEST NEED HERE: _____

_____

_____

_____

_____

WRITE YOUR NAME HERE: _____

_____

NOW SAY:

GOD'S SUPPLY ALWAYS EQUALS MY NEED

10 HOW GOD'S SUPPLY ALWAYS EQUALS YOUR NEED

THE LAW OF SUPPLY and demand in this country usually regulates the prices we have to pay for services and goods. If there is an oversupply, the price ordinarily goes down. If there is a shortage, the demand exceeds the supply and prices are forced up.

This problem has never been solved and perhaps never will be. People are frustrated by it. And when they accept the frustration as part of their lives, they deny that God's supply equals their need.

And that is exactly what too many people, including Christians, are doing today. Here's how you can change this:

The Blessing-Pact principle makes God your Source, not the law of supply and demand. It does not eliminate or bypass the law of supply and demand, but it is not limited by it in bringing God's supply for your needs.

GOD MEETS OUR NEEDS "ACCORDING TO HIS RICHES"

The principle of God as Source takes into account His riches. Paul says, "But my God shall supply all your need according to his riches in glory by Christ Jesus" (Philippians 4:19).

According to God's riches!

A man once did a good turn for a person he didn't know. Gratefully, the man he had helped hastily wrote a note, signed it, and handed it to him. A few years later, this man fell on hard times. Remembering the note, he went to the bank where the man who had written it was president.

"I've come to get my hundred dollars," he said.

The president replied, "What do you mean you came to get your hundred dollars?"

The man said, "You told me if I ever needed help to come to you and you would stake me to a hundred dollars."

"What proof do you have of that?" the banker asked.

"Right here," he said as he handed him the piece of paper. It read, "The bearer of this piece of paper is entitled to $100 on demand." It was signed by the president.

"Oh, yes," the banker smiled. "I remember. Step right this way. It's a pleasure. I always keep my promises."

Now God always keeps His promises. I spend much of my time and effort in answering people who come right out and say that God doesn't even know they exist or God has forgotten them, or their need is too big or too strange. Sometimes it's a financial need, or a marriage problem, or a food problem, or a problem with their children, their parents, or a loved one who is ill.

During a three-day period recently, I canceled all my appointments and went up in the Prayer Tower to pray for the prayer requests in my mail. The first 70 letters had 70 different needs! Here is a list of some of those needs:

To protect my son in Vietnam

For something that is wrong in my life

For my family to be saved

For money to pay my bills

That God will forgive me of sins I've committed

That I may get a raise

That I may find the right job
That I may have a secure future
For something good to happen to me
For my soul and body to be healed
For my marriage to be healed
For God to bless our rental property
For God to help me; I'm so lonely
For me to have enough to eat
For me to learn how to trust God more
For God to help me get a home
For a closer walk
For my needs to be met
For God to give me that wonderful feeling you have
   in your ministry.

GOD'S SUPPLY REMAINS STABLE

I thought: *There are not 70 different sources for the supply of these needs but only one: God. He has promised to meet all our needs "according to His riches."*

Not according to the size of your need but according to His riches, God will supply it.

Whether prices are high or low, jobs are plentiful or scarce, business is up or down, God's supply remains stable. His supply is here beside you, now.

God is as much God during times of oversupply as undersupply. He is the same God in good times or bad times. His supply is "according to his riches in glory by Christ Jesus."

You can get a hang-up at this point if you are not careful. You can say, "Salvation is for my soul, for my spiritual welfare, and to take me to heaven; I'm not supposed to expect God to help me financially or with my marriage, or with any of my hang-ups." You can say that so often that you cause your need to appear to exceed God's supply.

This is what Peter and his partner in the fishing business were saying. When business was at its worst and the supply the lowest, Jesus came to the fishermen at the Sea of Galilee saying, "First, lend Me your boat." Then, "Launch out into the deep and let down your net for a catch." Peter replied, "Lord, we have toiled all night and taken nothing."

In our language today, Jesus said, "Look, Men, I've heard how bad business is, jobs are scarce, money is in short supply. I have come to help you with your trade."

Peter replies, "What does He know about our trade? He has been a carpenter, a worker with wood. Now He's a prophet, a worker with men's souls. How can He feel concern for me, a worker with fish? How can He tell us how to catch fish or run our business?"

But when Peter obeyed and gave something to Jesus first and then looked to Him as the Source of his supply, he had a miracle! He discovered that Jesus is not only the Savior of the soul but He is Master over everything, including the fishing business.

Peter and his partners caught so many fish the nets couldn't hold them and their boat was too small to carry them away. They had to call neighbors in to share the catch! (Reread Chapter 3 of this book for further understanding of the miracle-catch.)

It's the same today when apparently for many people the law of supply and demand has dried up the sources for jobs, for business, and prosperity. A miracle can happen and you can have a choice of going to work at three or four good places, or seeing ways to expand in many different directions, or seeing your marriage healed and falling in love all over again, or gaining friends as never before, or seeing your son or daughter straighten out, or having your body renewed in health and strength, or your soul running over with joy, or finding your witness starting to work more effectively.

It's wonderful!

HOW AN ASSOCIATE OF MINE FACED A DIP IN THE STOCK MARKET

One of my associates, the only one of us who has an independent income, came in one day looking glum. This man has probably used his Blessing-Pact as successfully as anyone I know. That morning, however, he had failed to keep his mind on God, THE Source of his supply. He had it on the stock market which the previous several days had plummeted to the lowest point in four years.

A part of his estate was in stocks. He had looked forward to their growth and dividends for additional income when he retired. This also enabled him to work with us for a modest salary and without having to use his capital.

"What's the matter?" I asked him.

"What's the matter? Have you read the stock market report this morning? My losses are nearly 50 percent."

"As a Blessing-Pact partner, what difference does that make to you?"

"Well, it makes a lot of difference," he said. "The market is down; it's really hurting me. It's keeping me awake at night."

"Don't take your thoughts and create that kind of soil. God is your Source of supply, not the stock market."

"But," he replied, "that's where my earnings are."

"But your giving is with God. You're regularly giving seed-money to the Lord. Your very life-style has been giving. I've never known a more generous man. The seed you've been sowing is not dependent upon the stock market but upon your relationship with God. Don't multiply your doubts by your thoughts, multiply your faith."

Standing there before me he was really wrestling with

his intellect. The stock market was the repository of his earnings and from the natural point of view it was the source of his future financial security. The problem with this was that he was left to the mercy of the stock market, which is managed and manipulated by men. By the laws of men, the market will inevitably go up, and go down; it will never be completely stable. It's not in the nature of man for anything he does to be stable. Stability is in God.

My friend said, "If the market keeps going down, I could be wiped out."

I said, "Not if your trust is in God as your Source of supply. God controls all sources of supply, both the expected and unexpected sources. If you are wiped out from one source, God will give you a supply from another source. You cannot be wiped out or defeated for long if you continue to look to God as your Source."

As understanding dawned, he gave a sigh of relief. "This is the first time I've really understood this part of my Blessing-Pact," he said, "and it sure makes me feel good."

The negative act of taking his mind off the Lord and putting it on the fluctuating abilities of men and the markets could have reduced him to a case of ulcers and completely wiped him out both financially and spiritually.

I've watched this man through the years. And every year his confidence in God has grown. His witness for Christ has grown more effective. A deeper calm has come into his heart. Everywhere I go I meet people with whom he has shared these principles and they tell me how this has caused them to look to God as their Source.

when they saw Christ revealed, when they saw themselves with overwhelming needs, and when they finally recognized that having Christ meant He is the Source for all their needs to be met.

The first time I saw 3,000 people accept Christ in a single service was in Johannesburg, South Africa. These were mostly people of European extraction — Dutch, English, French, etc. When I held Christ up to them as EVERY-THING for their needs, they couldn't wait to come forward. The next night, 4,000 came forward, the final night, 5,000! I've seen it happen in Asia, South America, Europe, in the African Bush, and in so-called sophisticated America. One night in the Hollywood Bowl, 16,000 people poured in. I spoke on "The Fourth Man," giving the titles God gave His Son, Jesus, in every book of the Bible, and stressing how each title represents God's coming in the form of a person's needs today. More than 3,000 streamed forward to take Christ as their personal Savior and as Master of everything in their lives.

In having Jesus you can discover He is THE Way to every need ultimately being met.

Jesus Christ has become the whole of my existence. Not once have I felt the slightest desire to leave Him. This is true of every person I know who has met Christ in this way.

JESUS APPEARS IN DIFFERENT WAYS

Now what people see in Jesus Christ is not always the same. Different things about Him appeal to people. With me the sincere witness of my sister, "Oral, God is going to heal you," was His appeal to me. To my father, it was a sermon. My mother first felt her need of Christ through a gospel song. Many today are reached in other ways. But the person always feels Christ in the form of his need.

In dealing with people and their problems, I have been forced by necessity to discover things about Jesus Christ that work in the now, particularly as they relate to our needs in our earthly life.

This is true of doctors, lawyers, scientists, businessmen, and those in all the professions. A need has driven them to search further for answers.

Jesus said, "The children of this world are in their generation wiser than the children of light" (Luke 16:8). They are often more sensitive to human problems and finding solutions than Christians ordinarily are.

There is no doubt that Jesus placed the chief emphasis on man's need being met. In fact, He is the only One who was bold enough to say, "I am the way" to get that need met. He stated unequivocally that the Way is not a thing but a Person. That Person is himself.

HOW JESUS ATTRACTED ME

That the Christian way is Jesus Christ the Person is what attracted me to Him in the first place. My need was healing from tuberculosis and stammering. Fearing that I would die, many Christian friends of my parents who visited me prayed that I would be saved so I could go to heaven. How much their idea influenced me I do not know. What I remember that turned me around was an entirely different approach.

My sister, Jewel, rushed in one day and said, "Oral, God is going to heal you."

I said, "Is He, Jewel?"

She said, "Yes."

A whole new world came before me. In a flash I realized that if God were going to heal me, I was a person of value, not merely someone who was going to die with tuberculosis. He was concerned about me and wanted me to live. He cared for me in that moment and had revealed it through the faith my sister felt for me. He came to me in the form of my need. It was SEED-FAITH Jewel planted in my behalf.

A few weeks later God sent a man across my path who had faith to pray for me to be healed. By that time my own faith had crystallized and I was ready to release it toward God.

When Jewel first planted SEED-FAITH that God would heal me, I had thought very little of becoming a Christian. In my family one did not automatically think of himself as a Christian because he was reared to attend church or to be confirmed. It was an intensely personal matter. Each child had to come to Christ for himself, repent of his sins, and believe on the Lord Jesus Christ. There was a further personal step: receiving an infilling of the Holy Spirit.

There are many advantages in being reared in a Christian atmosphere. There can be disadvantages, too. For example, there can be the disadvantage of too much emphasis being placed on the crisis-moment of conversion. Not that this personal starting point can be overstressed. The problem comes when you fail to realize that birth is one thing and growth and understanding is another.

I don't think there is too much emphasis placed upon going "to" church. It is highly important to meet in a house of God with other believers to hear and study the Word of God and learn to apply Christian principles. The problem is failing to understand that Jesus also teaches that the Christian is to "go" into his community and become involved with the needs of people, and to learn to think of God as appearing in the form of the need a person has.

There is a "missing gap" between sitting in church and in coming to grips with the actual gritty problems we face in our physical existence outside the church services.

Another disadvantage can be in putting so much emphasis on going to heaven that you are not aware God expects you to use your faith to bring God's kingdom into the area of your present needs. As someone put it, "Don't be so heavenly minded that you are no earthly good."

Jesus showed His concern by teaching us in the Lord's Prayer to say, "Thy will be done in earth, as it is in heaven" (Matthew 6:10).

JESUS WAS EARTHBOUND

Do not forget that for 33 years Jesus was an earthbound Person. He employed the same principles of the Blessing-Pact to get His material needs met that I am referring to in SEED-FAITH.

1. He was always talking about His Father. "My Father and I are one." His Father was THE Source and Jesus was one with that Source.

2. Jesus' life-style was giving in the totality of himself. He spoke out of His own experience when He said, "Give and it shall be given to you," and, "It is more blessed to give than to receive." God loves a cheerful giver. Jesus had plumbed the depths of giving and found that whatever He gave was multiplied back again and again. He often demonstrated this.

3. In the wedding feast at Cana of Galilee, we see Jesus using the third principle of the Blessing-Pact — EXPECTING A MIRACLE. When He told the servants at the wedding feast at Cana of Galilee to fill the waterpots with water, He said, "Now, pour out." When He said, "Pour," He was expecting a miracle of the water being made into wine. (Read this story in John 2:1-11.)

108

When He told the fishermen to "Launch out into the deep and let down your nets for a catch," He was expecting them to miraculously catch a net-breaking, boat-sinking load in the same spot where they had already failed — and the miracle happened!

He said, "When ye ask, expect to receive."

I see Jesus as a Man who looked to God as THE Source, who practiced giving as a life-style and as SEED-FAITH, and who expected both natural and supernatural power to work in His behalf.

This is the person He wants you to be.

A rejected opportunity to give is a lost opportunity to receive. Jesus said, "Give, and it shall be given unto you..." Receiving follows giving. A miracle follows believing....The harvest follows seed-sowing and soil-tending.

12

HOW A FRIEND GOT HIS DREAM JOB THROUGH APPLYING THE KEY PRINCIPLES OF THE BLESSING-PACT

A FRIEND OF MINE had a job that required him to drive 120 miles round trip daily. Within walking distance of his home was a large plant which paid good wages and offered good working conditions. Besides saving wear and tear on his car and himself, if he worked there he could come home each day for lunch. For several years he had applied regularly for a job there but was turned down each time. During this period the company hired hundreds of new employees. He couldn't understand this and finally gave up.

One day he heard me speak on the key principles of the Blessing-Pact. I explained and gave examples of its three key principles:

First, look to God as the Source of your supply.

Second, give as seed-giving and it will become SEED-FAITH for God to multiply back in the form of your need.

Third, by looking to God as your Source, and giving as SEED-FAITH, this is evidence on which your faith can act — so expect a miracle of God's supply.

In my message I made a statement that turned this man and his wife around. Or, as they said later, "It turned us on."

The statement was this: <u>A rejected opportunity to give</u>

111

is a lost opportunity to receive.

This statement is in harmony with Jesus' statement in Luke 6:38, "Give, and it shall be given unto you; good measure, pressed down, and shaken together, and running over, shall men give into your bosom. For with the same measure that ye mete withal it shall be measured to you again."

RECEIVING FOLLOWS GIVING

They saw that receiving follows giving. A miracle follows believing. Breathing in follows breathing out. The harvest follows seed-sowing and soil-tending.

In 2 Corinthians 9:10 we read, "Now he that ministereth seed to the sower both minister bread for your food, and multiply your seed sown, and increase the fruits of your righteousness." In other words, God who gives you seed to sow is the One who multiplies the seed sown!

God gives you an opportunity to give, which if you accept it, turns into an opportunity for you to receive.

Well, this man and his wife accepted the Blessing-Pact Covenant and put in seed-money that very day to help do God's great work. Regularly, each month, they sent in seed-money. Meanwhile they were learning to look to God as their Source and to put Him first in their lives.

I think it was four months later that I had occasion to chat with them. An amazing story unfolded.

He had thought no more about applying to the plant as he had done several times before. He told me, "But one morning at breakfast, I felt something drawing me to apply again." He looked at his wife. She seemed to be experiencing the same feeling. "Oh, it's no use," he told her, "they'll just say, no, like before."

I said, "You were still in the old pattern, expecting nothing after being refused so many times. You still had your mind set that there was no further hope."

He said, "I had been working on my thoughts, to put them on God and to trust Him to open doors for me. It didn't come easy. Gradually my Blessing-Pact became real to me. God had become my Source. I was giving as Jesus told me to, and I knew God would start multiplying it back. How, I didn't know. But I knew He would do it in His own good time and way. I knew He would open the door to a different and better job — I was *expecting* it. But when I felt this urge to apply again at the plant near us, I was a little surprised. I hadn't expected God to work in that direction."

I said, "That's good that you didn't specify how God would do it. As your Source, He knows what's best."

He said, "I told my wife that I just couldn't go ask again, and dismissed it from my mind."

Then his wife remembered, *A rejected opportunity to give is a lost opportunity to receive.* She thought, *Our Blessing-Pact Covenant with God is based on the principle of trusting God as the Source of our supply, and for our guidance. We have been giving seed into His kingdom by helping His servant do God's work. We have both been expecting a miracle.* Then she said, "Well, why not?"

He said, "Well, why not what?"

She answered, "You've been wearing yourself and the car out driving 120 miles a day, just to hold down a job. God has something better for us. Our Blessing-Pact is up-to-date. That feeling we have is God starting to multiply our SEED-FAITH back to us."

Growing more excited she said, "I think you should go down there in the morning and go to work."

He said, "You know, her face shone. The Blessing-Pact was shining through. I felt the same way she did but her conviction about this encouraged me. So I told her I'd drive the 120 miles one more day, then I'd apply. If that door doesn't open, I know God will open another."

FIRST CLASS

Now I like to talk to people who are standing up on the inside. Something reaches out and grips me. I know they mean business with God. They are through accepting second or third best when God has only one class — FIRST CLASS.

I like to hear people say, "Well, why not? God is alive. He's here at the point of my need, I've given Him my best and I'm going to expect His best."

The way some people are going they are never going to get anywhere. They are like the woman who said, "I always feel the worst when I feel the best, because I know how bad I'm going to feel when I start feeling bad again."

Others are going to get up on the inside and start doing what God told them in His Word. They are going to change from looking to self or to men and start looking to God to move in on the scene. God is going to become their Source, all other forces will be instruments only. If one instrument fails, they will keep their mind on Him and expect Him to help through another instrument.

I admit I get excited about applying the Blessing-Pact principles.

My friend rose the next morning feeling as if he owned the world. He bowed his head at breakfast, gave thanks, ate, told his wife to keep looking up and strode off to the employment office of this plant near his home. Pretty soon he was back. Bounding through the door, he said, "Honey, I got the job!"

She said, "How? Tell me all about it."

He said, "When I walked in I told them my name and that I had come to go to work. The man actually acted as if he had been waiting for me. He told me they would be ready for me as soon as I could come. Then he signed me up and told me to hurry back and report to work."

Call this a coincidence, call it positive thinking, call it an accident. I call it the Blessing-Pact as SEED-FAITH in action! It proves God is where the need is, and when SEED-FAITH is sown God multiplies it back in the form of that need.

My friend said, "This is my dream job come true. The thing I like best is that I can walk to work and walk home for lunch if I like. Each day I give thanks to God, for truly He sent this miracle to us."

13

A VIETNAM VETERAN ASKS, "ORAL ROBERTS, WHAT PERSON DO YOU TURN TO WHEN YOU ARE IN A JAM?"

HE HAD JUST GOTTEN HOME from Vietnam. As fast as possible he had put his young wife in the car and had driven to Oral Roberts University here in Tulsa. With nearly 900 other students he was trying to get enrolled in time for the first classes.

With what the Government provided for his education, and what he could earn from a part-time job he still didn't have enough money to pay his way and support his wife at the same time. The University gave him some special assistance. Still he fell short.

He nearly panicked. He told someone, "Facing this is a lot tougher than Vietnam."

On his own now he was having to look life squarely in the face and get along as best he could.

"President Roberts," he said when he reached me, "can you help me?"

I asked what sources he had gone through. The Government, the University, his job, and even his family back home. "And I'm still short," he said. I knew the costs at ORU were not that high so I asked him to give me a breakdown of the costs and his own assets. I had to admit he had it figured close.

I asked him if he had heard of the Blessing-Pact or SEED-FAITH. He said, "No, what is it?" As I started explaining, he said, "What does that have to do with me? My problem is getting enough money together to get through college."

Then he said, "What person do I turn to now?"

I replied, "Have you tried the Person of Christ?"

He said, "Sure. Why do you think I'm here? My dream in Vietnam was to get out alive, come home for my wife, and enroll here at ORU. I believe in what you stand for. I want an education for the whole man. But what I must have is some money — soon."

At last he had gotten to the root of the matter. Money. The medium of exchange. He had gone from source to source and he was getting frantic. It had not yet dawned on him that Jesus was concerned about the money. Jesus had been with him in Vietnam, had helped him hold to the dream of being a student at Oral Roberts University, had made it possible for him to be here right now. He believed this, had exercised faith for it, now his faith was being directed to a source quite different — man. Oh, he was not aware that in this financial need he had turned away from God, his Source in Vietnam, and who had brought him to this campus. But that is what he had done.

I have done this many times and I recognize it in others. I said, "It appears the University has done all it can do. If you will take a few moments for me to share some thoughts on God, your Source, on giving as seed-money, and on expecting a miracle, this need can be met."

We were not on the same wavelength. He blurted, "Oral Roberts, what person do you turn to when you are in a jam?"

I replied, "What person? You mean, what man?"

He said, "Yes."

117

I thought a moment, *What person do I turn to when I am in a jam?* It's been so long since I turned to one, I can't think of any. Finally I said, "No one."

"Well, who do you turn to?" he asked.

I said, "God. Every time I have turned to Him and applied the principles of the Blessing-Pact I have found a supply for my needs. Only in those times that I have sought man rather than God have I failed."

He said, "You mean you don't have a person to turn to?"

"None that I know of," I said.

"That's bad."

"No, it's great!"

"Why do you say that?" he asked.

GOD NEVER FAILS TO ANSWER IN TIME

I said, "Because my Blessing-Pact starts with God. It always works. Not always as quick or in the form I expect, but when I really turn to Jesus Christ as a Person and apply the principles of the Blessing-Pact, God has never failed to answer in time. It always works."

This young man thought I was talking in riddles. He had heard preachers warn of material things. Now that he was face-to-face with the need of an amount of money to exchange for his education, he didn't know that God expected him to use his faith for this in the same way he had done to go through the Vietnam War and come home safely. It was the gap between being saved and at the end of life, heaven.

I said, "You're a new student, aren't you?"

"Yes."

"I know all students have needs, financial and otherwise. Tonight I am meeting with all new students and speaking to them on how to apply the Blessing-Pact to get their needs met. Can you be there?"

He said, "It's required, isn't it? I'll be there."

I laughed. "It's part of the orientation of new students. However, you won't be required to accept everything I say."

"I'll be there," he said.

GIVING AS A LIFE-STYLE

That evening I shared some of the things in this book, applying them to the student level. They were excited about the idea of God in the now, about God's being concerned with them as a person, and concerned with both their spiritual and material needs. I shared how to make God THE Source, and all others as instruments God would use; how to give as a life-style, sowing SEED-FAITH for God to multiply to help others and themselves; and how to develop a frame of mind of expectancy for God to come to them in the form of their need, and to recognize and receive it.

I find it thrilling to talk to young people about SEED-FAITH in the Blessing-Pact. They lay hold of it almost instantly.

At the close of the session, several gathered around to ask questions and share thoughts of their own. Suddenly the young Vietnam veteran shoved his hand forward, grasped mine and said, "Sir, I don't need to rely on you anymore. I've found my Source. He and I can handle it. Thank you."

I said, "As you do this, and you find the way to carry these principles over into your future life and family, you will really learn how to live."

Don't misunderstand me. Don't think I am referring only to money. People with money are often the poorest people in the world.

A FAITH TO PASS ON

Recently, a man sat down beside me in an airplane I was

traveling on. He said, "Where are you from?"

I said, "Tulsa."

"What's your name?"

"Oral Roberts."

"Oh, I've been wanting to talk to you."

I wondered why, since he was partly drunk. When the stewardess came with cocktails, he asked for a double amount. He wanted to talk about my philosophy on life, asking me how I got started, how I made business decisions, and what I thought was the number one thing in life.

Finally, I asked him a question: "What is your goal in life?"

With all his might he tried to focus his eyes and get control of himself. Turning his gaze on me, he said, "My goal in life is to earn enough money to pass on to my sons."

He didn't know that I knew of him. He was one of the wealthiest men in the Southwest. I said, "You're going to make your sons pretty rich, then."

He said, "Yeah."

I said, "What else are you leaving them?"

He said, "I don't know. I hadn't thought about it."

When we landed we had to assist him to get his luggage and find transportation to the city. As he went weaving and wobbling to the cab, I remembered the young veteran. Compared to this man, he was poor in material things but the veteran had found the Source. He knew that together, he and God could handle his needs. In addition, he had a faith he could pass on to his sons that would make them truly rich.

I recall a conversation I heard a number of years ago between my father and one of his brothers. My uncle said, "Ellis, I would give all I possess if I could step out of my shoes into yours."

My father said, "What do you mean?"

He replied, "I've given my children everything that money can buy and they have broken my heart. You have not had too much money to give to your children. But you have given them something money cannot buy. You have given them an example of rich faith in God."

That night family prayer suddenly meant a lot more to me.

PART III

IS YOUR BLESSING-PACT WORKING?
HERE'S HOW TO CHECK YOURSELF

14

WHEN IT DOESN'T SEEM TO WORK— HOW TO CHECK YOURSELF ON THE THREE KEY PRINCIPLES OF THE BLESSING-PACT

A PARTNER ONCE WROTE ME of his disappointment in using the Blessing-Pact principle.

"Nothing is going right," he said. "The company has decided it can't use me anymore. Here I am without a position and with no promise of one with another company. Everyone is letting me down. My finances have never been worse. What is wrong with my Blessing-Pact?"

I could almost feel the knot of fear in his stomach and the doubt taking root in his mind. What I feared most was that now he was beginning to sow seed that would be multiplied back in the form of more fear, more doubt, more disillusionment.

I remembered an incident in Tulsa. I was driving through a 15-mile-an-hour school zone. The elderly gentleman who was watching out for the children and keeping the motorists within the speed limit threw up his flag and pulled me over.

"I calculate you were going about 20 miles an hour, 5 over the limit."

I said, "I guess I'd better have my speedometer checked."

"Mister," he said, "have you ever had yourself checked?"

I got the point.

I wrote my friend, "You are asking what's wrong with

your Blessing-Pact. Why not check yourself?"

I asked that he ask himself three questions:

1. Am I looking to God as THE Source for my employment?
2. Am I giving as SEED-FAITH for God to multiply?
3. Am I expecting a miracle?

WHAT HE DISCOVERED

He checked himself with these questions and was astonished at what he discovered.

The first discovery was that he really was not giving. This aspect of the Blessing-Pact had been an ideal to him. He had subconsciously used the tithing principle rather than giving first as Jesus said.

Also he was waiting until he earned a lot, then he was going to give the tithe of it. Of the amount he already had earned, he had given nothing. There is a certain sense of obligation in tithing, a feeling of a debt owed. It requires obedience and gratitude. I wonder if this is why some never get around to paying their tithes.

I told my friend that Jesus wanted to bring him into an attitude of joy in giving, then he would not feel so much an obligation but a great opportunity for God to take what he gave and multiply it to help others, and then give back to him. I said, "You've got to start. Just take the amount that you feel the Lord lays on your heart, think of it as seed, and give it cheerfully. As day follows night, receiving follows giving. You'll get your harvest and you'll know a joy you've never felt before."

The next discovery was that he had not applied Jesus' teaching on THE Source. The Bible says, "But my God shall supply all your need according to his riches in glory by Christ Jesus" (Philippians 4:19).

I said, "Here you are with your mind on the means rather than THE Source. You have been looking to the company you were working for as THE Source for all your supply, not God. Now you are trying to think of another company so you can repeat the same process and make the same mistake again."

In the past, I had done the same thing so many times that I recognized that this was his problem.

Therefore, he had no evidence on which to base his faith for another job that would be the right job. He had failed in the past to sow SEED-FAITH and now he could not expect a miracle. There was no basis for it — no seed — no harvest.

The worst part was he didn't realize he was failing to sow SEED-FAITH. Consequently, he was going in a vicious circle. Oh, he was sowing seed. But it was bad seed. It was seed-doubt, the counter principle of SEED-FAITH. Whether we sow seed-doubt or SEED-FAITH, the principle remains, we will reap what we sow. (See Galatians 6:7; 2 Corinthians 9:6.)

As I shared these thoughts with him, he said, "Oh, yes, I see. I was waiting to receive before I started giving. I was not looking to God as my Source. Now I see that miracles don't happen outside of God and doing what He says."

He got his thinking straightened out and the principles of the Blessing-Pact have begun to work in his life.

EVELYN CHECKS HERSELF

While I was writing this book, Evelyn, my wife, was doing some proofreading for me and she stopped and said: "Oral, here where you refer to expecting a miracle — it's at this point that I need to check myself with my Blessing-Pact. I've missed it here several times."

I said, "Honey, I guess we all have. But we've got to take Jesus at His Word. Jesus will either do what He said or He is the biggest liar ever born."

She said, "Well, we know His Word is true."

I said, "Look, if I say I am sending you something and inwardly you say that you don't believe it, then when it arrives you may not be home to receive it. It comes; you are not there. You never know it came and you continue to doubt. Now Jesus can't force a miracle upon us, or force us to expect it or to receive it. After we do what He has told us to do, doing it sincerely and in faith, we know He will send a miracle. We know it, so let's expect it."

Evelyn said, "Yes, and I'm going to do a lot more expecting from God in the future."

A COACH PUTS ME ON THE SPOT

The Blessing-Pact is something I can check myself with constantly. I find I need to. If I don't I get busy and neglect it. Then I wonder why God is not answering.

"Mr. Roberts, I've heard you make that statement several times," said a friend, who is a coach, "that you have to continually check yourself. Well — what about a fellow like me?"

I said, "What do you mean?"

He replied, "You're doing the Lord's work all the time. I can see that if it's hard for you to remember to check yourself with the Blessing-Pact, it's going to be a lot harder for me."

I said, "Well, maybe so, maybe not. I find I check myself more often when I really realize that outside of God I have no other Source. You can't depend on all the people you deal with. You can't even depend on yourself always. But you can depend on Him who is our eternal Source of supply."

He replied, "Well, I'm sure going to start checking myself more often. Coaches need the Blessing-Pact, too."

I said, "Doesn't everybody?"

It is very important <u>how</u> you give. If it is money...it is neither good nor bad except as you are... it reflects you in your total self. There's nothing you can do with the gift once you've given it. But there is everything you can do with your attitude and spirit of expectancy.

15

HOW THE SPIRIT OF YOUR GIVING INFLUENCES YOUR RECEIVING

THE SPIRIT in which you give is the most important part of giving. It is very important *how* you give.

If it is money, the gift is inanimate — a piece of money. It is a medium of exchange only. It is neither good nor bad except as you are. You clothe it in your spirit; it reflects you in your total self.

I often think a sign, "HANDLE WITH CARE," or "HANDLE WITH PRAYER," should be near when you give.

There's nothing you can do with the gift once you've given it. But there is everything you can do with your attitude and spirit of expectancy.

YOU MUST BOTH PLANT THE SEED AND CULTIVATE THE SOIL

You learn through the Blessing-Pact principle that God expects you to both plant the seed and cultivate the soil. The seed is your giving; the soil is your personal relationship with Christ. Without this personal relationship your giving will profit you nothing.

Paul says, "Though I bestow all my goods to feed the poor . . . and have not love [Jesus], it profiteth me nothing." In other words, the spirit of your giving reflects your lifestyle. (Turn to 1 Corinthians 13 and read what Paul says

129

about seed-love.)

Remember, when the farmer plants seed, he gives the best seed he has. Then he continues to work with the soil. He no longer works with the seed. Once the seed is planted that is all he can do with it. It is the soil the seed has to grow in that is of continuing concern to him.

"Well, after I give," a man said to me, "isn't that all I can do? Isn't that my part?"

I said, "It's true that the seed you sow is what God will multiply back. But the seed cannot grow unless it is good seed, and it cannot grow in soil that is no longer tended. The harvest will either be small or nothing at all. If in your giving you continue to cultivate your personal relationship with God — which is tending the soil — you can rightfully expect a good harvest."

Jesus gives two illustrations of this principle: the first concerns the type of soil and how it is tended; the other, the abundance of the harvest.

In Luke 8:5-8 He gave the parable of the sower. He said, "A sower went out to sow his seed: and as he sowed, some fell by the way side; and it was trodden down, and the fowls of the air devoured it. And some fell upon a rock; and as soon as it was sprung up, it withered away, because it lacked moisture. And some fell among thorns; and the thorns sprang up with it, and choked it. And other fell on good ground, and sprang up, and bare fruit an hundredfold."

The seed the sower used was good seed but how and where he sowed it determined the amount of harvest.

First, consider the seed sowed by the wayside. This was uncultivated soil. He paid attention only to the seed. It bore no fruit. Next, the seed carelessly sowed on rocky soil. The soil had no depth nor could it hold moisture. No fruit. The next seed was sowed among thorns and weeds which already had their growth and thus smothered the seed. Result: no fruit. Finally, the sower learned his lesson. He sowed only in soil he had carefully prepared and continued to cultivate. There was a 100 percent harvest.

"Are you saying," a man asked, "that what I give can result in nothing?"

"Yes, that's what I'm saying," I replied. "I've seen it happen."

Occasionally people have tried to offer me money to pray for a loved one. They thought they could buy prayer as they could something in the marketplace. At the beginning of this ministry I made a vow: "I will touch neither the gold nor the glory." I have kept that vow. I've never received a private gift in connection with my prayers for a person, and in every instance when a healing or other blessing came I knew God did it and I said so.

GOD CONSIDERS YOUR ATTITUDE

Friend, when you are dealing with God, it is always your attitude He considers. Not that you can get so good that you are worthy. None of us are worthy.

I recall a person who virtually forced me to pray for her after a service in which I had become exhausted. Finally, in anger, I touched her. To my amazement, she received healing. She went away rejoicing; I went away perplexed. I am afraid I touched her to get her out of my way so I could get to my room and get some rest. But she took my touch as her point of contact, released her faith to God, and was healed. Later as I lay down God whispered in my heart: "I healed her but you won't receive any credit for it." I had given in anger; therefore, that was the seed I sowed. Thus God became displeased with me. There had

131

been no joy in my giving, hence there was none when I saw her recover.

The many lessons I've learned the hard way along these lines are too numerous to mention. There is one thing certain, if you and I are going to know joy in receiving we must first experience joy in our giving. And we can.

16 WHY I SELECTED AND GAVE MY LARGEST BILL

A WOMAN HEARD ME SPEAK on the Blessing-Pact at the International Convention of the Full Gospel Business Men. I had said, "In the Blessing-Pact you look to God and put Him first in everything, including your giving. What you give is seed-giving for God to use to help others and to multiply back to you. When you give, remember, give God your best, then ask Him for His best. The greater the sacrifice, the greater the blessing. Jesus says, 'For with the same measure that ye mete withal, it shall be measured to you again.'"

She told me later, "As the offering was being taken for the convention, I opened my purse and selected one of the smaller bills. Then I remembered your talk to give to God my best, then ask Him for His best and with what measure I give, it will be measured to me again. I decided to prove this to myself. I returned the smaller bill and selected the largest one and gave it."

I said, "This was the first time you had heard of the Blessing-Pact principle?"

She said, "Yes, and it was exciting."

I said, "Did you get the proof you wanted?"

She said, "Oh, I certainly did. First, going from the

The greater the sacrifice, the greater the blessing. Jesus said, "For with the same measure that ye mete withal it shall be measured to you again" habit of offering only my smallest bill to the Lord to my largest was a big bridge for me to cross. After I had found the faith and courage to do it, I was perfectly delighted. I had given my best and, for the first time, I felt I knew a little of how God felt when He gave His only begotten Son, His very best gift."

Then, with a twinkle in her eyes, she said, "I put the little bill back and selected the largest bill in my purse. You see, I have a big need."

I said, "You can't miss."

She said, "This has really turned me around. As you say, 'Something GOOD is going to happen to me.'"

I TOOK MY PROBLEM TO CHURCH

I was sitting in church one Sunday morning recently. A problem was on my mind. Several people had applied for a certain position on my team, but each time when a decision was to be made something always happened. We were at the deadline and we were no nearer a solution.

I don't know of a better place to take your problems than to the House of God. One part of me was listening to the beautiful hymns and the other part was praying for God to send us His man. The Blessing-Pact had been involved in all my dealings with the various applicants. Instead of trying to settle on one, I endeavored to keep my mind open to God as the Source for the right person, the key one. Sitting there, I became aware that the offering trays were being passed. What happened next almost caused me to miss applying the Blessing-Pact in the one area I had, so far, not done in order to completely release my faith. Automatically, I guess, I took my wallet out and selected a bill. The church I was in was not my home church and, although I always love to give something anywhere I worship, I ordinarily give a larger amount at my local church.

Suddenly a feeling came over me, *Give your largest bill.* I found myself reacting, "I should write a check so we can secure a tax deduction. If I give a larger amount in cash, they probably will disallow it on our tax return."

Sounds foolish, doesn't it, for me to be sitting in God's House carrying on a conversation with myself like that? Well, I did.

For some reason the ushers were delayed in reaching our section. While debating on what I should do, another thought came. *Give God your largest bill, then ask Him for the best man for this position and expect the answer soon.*

A KNOWING CAME IN MY HEART

That settled the matter. I realized God was activating the Blessing-Pact to help me get this need met and, tax deduction or not, I was moving with God. I selected my largest bill and folded it so the ushers could not tell what it was and dropped it in the offering. I felt a flow and a knowing come into my heart. I knew. It was faith and mine was being released.

When the service was over I left there feeling mighty good. Through my gift I had invested SEED-FAITH for God to multiply back. I was able to move with confidence and soon we had our man.

I didn't know as I sat there deciding between my smallest and largest bill that the man we felt was right for the job and who felt right about it himself, had gone to bed the previous night deciding not to come.

The next morning, while I was sitting there in church, he and his family were watching our TV program. As he related this to me several weeks later, it dawned on me that I was giving my largest bill and he was watching the TV program at approximately the same time! He said, "After the program was over I turned to my wife and said, 'Honey, we're going.' She said, 'Fine.' My two children spoke up, 'Dad, we're so glad. We wanted you to all the time.'"

He said, "Although it meant a move of nearly a thousand miles, the entire family felt real good about it, and I do too."

The only unit of time God recognizes is the <u>now</u>....With God this moment is the most important moment in your life. It is now that He will multiply back what you give to Him — whether it's love, faith, money, or any other good thing. It is <u>now</u> that He wants to give you a miracle.

17 WHEN NEED AFTER NEED FACES YOU — HERE'S WHAT TO DO

EVERYBODY HAS NEEDS. You do; I do. You will always have needs. When one is met, another will take its place. That's the way it is in this earthly life and will be until you get to heaven. Therefore, your Blessing-Pact Covenant is always important to you. Here are ways it can help you.

The Blessing-Pact Covenant as SEED-FAITH can help you to focus upon God as the Source of your supply. It can help you to keep giving as seed for an abundant harvest. It can help you to expect a miracle. Then the title of this book will be more than mere words — it will be *your* MIRACLE OF SEED-FAITH.

LIKE BEGETS LIKE

I knew an elderly woman whose Blessing-Pact changed her whole life-pattern. She had been in a vicious circle of being need-centered. We shared with her the Bible principle that "like begets like." Needs can multiply too when you are need-centered.

I've never seen a person more excited than she was when she first heard of the Blessing-Pact. She saw she could become God-centered which is to be answer-centered. She had not known Philippians 4:19 was in the Bible although she had grown up in the church. She went around quoting it to herself, "But my God shall supply all your need according to his riches in glory by Christ Jesus." Finally she inserted her name in this verse. "But my God shall supply all your need — Emma — according to his riches in glory by Christ Jesus."

She did the same thing with Luke 6:38, "Give, and it shall be given unto you; good measure, pressed down, and shaken together, and running over, shall men give into your bosom. For with the same measure that ye mete withal it shall be measured to you again." Then she added her name, involving herself in it and making it speak directly to her as a person with needs.

She said, "If I, Emma, will give, as Jesus said, it shall be given to me. I give before I receive. The hole I give through is the hole I get through. I can make it big or small. But I must give something to God first."

(Now read again the preceding three paragraphs and insert your name.)

Then she said, "I must have miracles, especially at my age. Because life is nearly over for me and I feel lonely and depressed, I have magnified my needs until all I am getting back is more needs. I must turn myself around and look to God as the Source of my supply. When I think of my needs it must be in terms of God's meeting them according to His riches. Then I must give and start expecting a miracle."

She told me, "The first benefit of my Blessing-Pact was with my children. The next time they came I sensed their fear that this visit would be a dreary one and they were hoping it would pass quickly. I was so full of joy, however, I couldn't contain myself. The running over had come to me, in my heart, and outwardly, too. I began sharing this with them. They looked at one another and wondered if this was their mother. When it was time to leave they asked if I had any needs they could help me with. I told them, no, everything was just great."

She said, "Oh, I continue to have my ups and downs but the ups are more than the downs. The children have begun bringing me things and now we have had some glorious times together."

The Blessing-Pact helped her because the Bible says, "It is more blessed to give than to receive" (Acts 20:35). It is what you give that God multiples back to you, not what you receive. Therefore, the greater blessing is in giving.

DON'T THINK THAT GETTING SAVED SOLVES EVERYTHING

It is so easy for someone to say, "Get saved so you can be happy and go to heaven when you die." Thank God that we can be saved, and that when we die, we can go to heaven, but there's more! There is more!

Some of the most need-centered and miserable people I know are saved people. They are loyal to their church, they give every Sunday, they live good lives morally, they pray, they do many good works, but are they happy? No, they are very unhappy.

They don't know how to deal with their problems and needs here on earth between the time they get saved and the time when they will go to heaven. It's in the life-span that we must have answers to our problems; in heaven we won't have needs.

In this life there are spiritual needs, physical needs, financial needs, social needs. The need of a car, house, furniture, food, insurance, medical care, clothes, marriage, children, job, health, security, safety, protection, loving care, order, calmness, rest, savings, friends, career, getting along with people, promotion, moving to another area, change — these and many more.

I have heard Christians cry, "Why has this happened to me? What have I done to deserve it?" They act surprised when trouble strikes. When needs get out of hand, when persecution comes, or when things don't go right they often lose their control.

It's very easy to develop an unconscious resentment toward God. In fact, many Christians actually believe that God sends sickness and other bad things on them. Hence, they believe it is not His will to heal or deliver them. They see their needs but don't feel God is concerned and doubt that it is His will to meet their needs.

This belief often makes them doubly confused and filled with guilt feelings. For example, sickness strikes. There is very little thought about asking God for healing. Oh, they may pray, "If it be Thy will, Lord, heal." While this type of practice is going on they call the doctor or go to him. They want to get well even if it takes an operation.

Here a person develops ambivalent feelings. One part of him has no real belief God wants to heal him. The other part anxiously calls for healing from medical science. He doesn't seem to realize this desire to be well is from God. Another thing this type of Christian does all too often is to separate healing into divine and human and make them exist poles apart.

But, you see, Jesus disagrees with this. In the Lord's Prayer He taught us to pray, "Thy will be done in earth as it is in heaven." If it is God's will for you to be well in heaven, it is His will for it on earth. Therefore, God is on the side of health. He heals both naturally and supernaturally, and seeks to make you whole.

God often heals through medical means. He heals

through climate; He heals through love and understanding; He heals through faith and prayer. If God heals you by medicine, or faith, it is all from Him, and to Him belongs the glory.

Your Blessing-Pact Covenant is very effective at this point in your life. In fact, from the moment you are saved until you go to heaven, the Blessing-Pact is designed to help you get your needs met.

Your Blessing-Pact says, "God is Source." It says, "God is first." It says, "Give first." It says, "Expect a miracle."

When Jesus spoke of being made whole it was always in the NOW. The only unit of time God recognizes is the *now*. It is in this moment that God is working. Therefore, with God this moment is the most important moment in your life. It is *now* that He will multiply back what you give to Him — whether it's love, faith, money, or any other good thing. It is *now* that He wants to give you a miracle.

DON'T COUNT YOURSELF OUT

The person who is having it hard says, "It's no use, I can't make it."

He has counted himself out. He has also counted out the Blessing-Pact. He will not get up until he realizes that God's miraculous return to him is his giving multiplied back by God.

One of the most negative men I ever met was a dedicated Christian, a hard worker, and a good man. When I met him he was selling home products door-to-door. He had brought his wife and small children to our crusade in Miami, Fla. We had one day off from the crusade so we went swimming in the Atlantic Ocean. He wanted to talk. He started in about how hard it was to make a living and get ahead. He told what some people had done to him.

The Blessing-Pact is designed to help you get your needs met. Your Blessing-Pact says, "God is Source." It says, "God is first." It says, "Give first." It says, "Expect a miracle."

He said that his sales were off, people were harder to deal with or sell to than ever before. He was having problems with some of the people in his church. Then like a record on an automatic record player he said over and over again, "It's no use, I can't make it."

That's when he got my attention. While he was detailing his problems and needs I knew there was nothing I could say or do to help. I had to wait until he ran down and came to the conclusion of being need-centered and say, "It's no use, I can't make it." It was at this moment that I might be able to show him he had sowed seeds of doubt that brought him a harvest of needs, and more needs.

I had not heard him say one positive thing. Not once had he spoken of God, or faith, or giving, or miracles. He wasn't "with it" as Jesus teaches.

He was not living in the *now* but in the *past*. He spoke of bills piling up, of a future looking darker, of people who had let him down, of failure in selling, of needs getting greater. Every breath was a negative one; he was caught up in it, and not aware that he had used the precious moments of our visit wholly in a negative way.

He was not aware of the principles of the Blessing-Pact. According to Jesus, your needs exist to be met. He teaches that your needs are your claim upon His concern for you as a person and His miracle-working power to be put to work in your behalf to meet those needs.

The Bible teaches, "All that I have is [yours] thine." — Luke 15:31

"Give, and it shall be given unto you." — Luke 6:38

"My God shall supply all your need." — Philippians 4:19

When you ask, expect to receive, or expect a miracle. — See Matthew 21:22

Jesus taught you are what your believing is. He said,

"As thou hast believed, so be it done unto thee" (Matthew 8:13).

Your believing can take opposite forms. It can be faith or it can be doubt.

When you believe God exists, that God loves you, and wants to meet your needs, that God is the Source of your supply, and therefore should be first in your life; when you believe that all God has is yours, when you start being like God by always giving first; when you believe that what you invest with God He will multiply back to you; when you believe you can come to God and He will receive you, then your believing has created *faith* in your heart.

With faith you do something *first* and thereby make your faith an act and release it toward God. In this way you actually demonstrate faith. You release the most positive and powerful thing in the universe — your faith. This is when you are really connected with God and make *contact* with the power that spins the universe and controls all things that affect you.

On the other hand, doubt is just as real, in a negative way, as faith. Doubt (or unbelief) is the REVERSED FORM of faith. It's when you believe God doesn't exist. Or, if you believe He exists, you believe He is not concerned with you as a person; He is not concerned with your needs. You believe what man can do is more reliable than what God will do. You believe that it's not up to God at all but what people do to you or you do yourself. You believe your main duty is to look out for number one — self — and you put God second or last in your scale of values and your approach to your needs. You believe that human forces are sources rather than God.

Through doubt you become very positive in your believing but in a reversed form. You are taking your capacity to believe and reversing it in a negative way. You say in effect, "It's no use, I can't make it." You expect no miracles. You say, "If God is love and power and help in time of need, He is certainly not concerned about me."

This is doubt and unbelief. It is bad, very bad for you. As SEED-FAITH is multiplied back, so is SEED-DOUBT.

This pattern of thinking and believing that you have created over the years keeps God from being real to you. Frankly, He is not real to you at all. Through this act of your believing, more doubt is multiplied back to you.

It's like a driver in a car. With the same hand he shifts to put the car in forward or reverse gear — same car, same gears, same driver — he causes the car to go in a different direction, forward or backward.

The Bible says, "God hath dealt to every man the measure of faith" (Romans 12:3). This God-given power to believe can create faith or doubt, depending upon the way you choose to believe. You can believe right by looking to God as your Source of all things, by putting Him first in your giving, and by expecting a miracle. When you do this, it WILL BECOME AN ACT OF FAITH which you can release toward God and which will bring you into a state of knowing. It makes you absolutely positive. It is SEED-FAITH.

Releasing this faith from your heart to God will release His mighty power within you. You will be brought to the peak of your abilities and be able to attract good things. You will become part of the solution rather than the problem. It puts your mind on God and His limitless resources rather than on the limited resources of mere mortal man.

You can believe wrong by looking to man rather than God as Source, and this becomes an act of your believing and creates doubt in your heart toward God. You can think

147

of what you are going to receive, rather than what you can give. In this negative spirit, you block the flow of God's intervention in your behalf to turn the tide.

Doubt cuts you off from the sources of unexpected supply. God controls both the expected and unexpected source, you know.

That day as we swam in the ocean and my friend finally wound down and said, "It's no use, I can't do it." I looked at him and said, "God didn't make you for this."

There was a little jerk in his body and he replied, "God didn't make me for what?"

"To use your believing to become completely negative," I said.

He answered, "Why, I never thought I was being negative."

I said, "There you have it. You are like thousands who are in the same spot you're in but never consider that they are negative persons. Their belief in God is never used for anything but to be saved and go to heaven. They don't believe that God will meet their needs in this life. They are negative where they should be positively believing God to help them now."

His mouth dropped open. I said, "You're a long time on this earth. You continually have problems and needs. It's time you recognized that the God who saved your soul, and who will someday take you to heaven, is the God of today. He is God in the now, in this moment of your existence. He loves you. He's concerned with your concerns. He can give you a whole new life if you will start this moment doing something first."

I didn't think he heard me. While the waves came in and out he stood there looking at me. After a while he said, "Oral Roberts, do you really believe what you are saying?"

"With all my heart," I replied.

"You don't know me," he said. "You don't know what has happened to me."

"Yes, I do," I laughed. "You've spent the last hour or two telling me."

Again he just stood and looked at me. "Let's go sit down on the beach," I suggested.

As we sat down, he said, "Help me."

I felt it when he said it. What a good feeling this is. You can only get help when you are ready and when you ask.

I said, "I want to ask you some questions. God can help you but He must have your wholehearted cooperation." In substance, here's what I asked.

"Who do you trust in?"

"Well, God, of course."

"Pardon me, but listening to you I didn't get that idea at all."

"I've been a Christian for a long time."

"I'm sure of that. But you were talking about needs and problems with your job, with people you deal with, with your family, with earthly things that are necessary to your existence. What I mean is, in all these things who do you trust in?"

Slowly, he said, "I guess I have never thought much about it."

You see, he had never thought of God in terms of meeting these needs in his life and family. I said, "I met God first when I learned He was concerned about my body. Through the possibility of healing for my body I became interested in God saving my soul. Then 12 years later when I learned God was interested in prospering His people, of meeting all their needs — spiritual, physical, and financial —

I became concerned about all these things too. Out of this has developed this ministry of healing for the whole man."

He said, "Well, being in your crusade is different from anything I've ever seen. Before I heard you, I hadn't been taught it is God's will to heal, or that we are supposed to expect miracles. A lot of my religious background has been in don'ts — don't do this, don't do that. I never heard a man say, 'God is a good God,' until I heard you say it. It's almost more than I can take in."

I said, "The same God who is the Source of your salvation and eternal life in heaven is also the Source for your other needs to be supplied. God is concerned about your spiritual development, and He is concerned with your financial needs as you peddle door-to-door. He's there too."

"Go on," he said.

"Do you give to the Lord?"

He said, "Oh, yes, I believe in tithing. I give a tenth to my church. I owe this to the Lord."

I said, "But do you ever release your faith when you give so God can give to you?"

He said, "Well, when you owe the Lord something, you just pay it."

I saw that he did not connect faith with his giving. It was done as a duty, an obligation, and without faith for a return. Again he had separated God from every part of his life except his being saved and going to heaven. God was back in the past when He saved his soul; He would be in heaven when he died and went there. But where is God in the NOW? Where is God this moment here when a man is down and feels he can never get up? Where is God when a man is saved, but is miserable and unhappy and too defeated in his battle with life to take care of his family and fulfill himself? The Scripture came to my mind,

"Jesus Christ the same yesterday, and to day and for ever" (Hebrews 13:8). I thought of the statement of Martha to Jesus concerning raising her brother Lazarus from the dead — "I know that he shall rise again in the resurrection at the last day. Jesus said unto her, I am the resurrection, and the life" (John 11:24,25).

I am!

Jesus didn't say, "I was."

He didn't say, "I shall be."

He said, "I am."

In every moment He is the great I am. He fills the now with himself. And that's where He comes to us, and we meet Him in the now.

Turning to my friend again, I asked, "In your job, your dealings with people, and all that, do you ever expect a miracle?"

He said, "I've only heard about doing that since I came down here. It's a new thought to me."

I said, "Look here. Listen. Do what I tell you from God's Word. I want you to straighten up, square your shoulders, and start a new beginning. I want you to return home looking to God and trusting Him as THE Source to supply your needs. I want you to give as you plant a seed and as a point of contact, and I want you to expect God to return it from unexpected sources. And as you go about your work, expect a miracle. I promise you if you will do these three things from your heart, and do them day in and day out, God will make you into a new man. You will prosper. Someday you won't know yourself. You may even own your own business. You will be in control of yourself. You will be an effective witness for Christ. You will have influence and fulfillment."

The rest of the day he was quiet. I caught him looking

far away several times, and then the day ended.

There was no way I could tell the impact of the Blessing-Pact principles made on him. As he said a few years later, "I had been down so long, getting up had never occurred to me." It took months for even a part of SEED-FAITH to soak in and become a part of his thinking. Every now and then a portion of it would become clear to him. Each time though he started putting it into practice.

The most amazing thing to me was when he came to a partners conference later in Tulsa. One look at him and I said, "What has happened to you?" He replied, "You should know."

He had come in a new car. He had on a nice-looking suit. He grabbed my hand in a positive way. He spoke without hesitating. He acted like a man on a mission.

He had not told me yet that he was no longer peddling from door-to-door. Nor did I know that he had started a little company of his own; his sons were in it with him. He had moved into a new home. He no longer was paying his tithes because of the sense of obligation; he was now giving with a joy and gladness, knowing God would multiply it back over and over. He had begun witnessing for Christ. Some miracles had been happening. Then he told me that he was at this conference to get more "ammunition."

Since then he has shared with me on several occasions. He is demonstrating the principles Jesus gave us in the Blessing-Pact in a practical way in the city where he lives, his church, his association with other people, and in the partnership he has with this ministry.

You cannot help but be inspired by a man who has come so far upward after he had said, "It's no use, I can't make it."

18

LET'S YOU AND ME HAVE A HEART-TO-HEART TALK THAT CAN HELP YOU

MY MAIL IS QUITE HEAVY these days. Every day people write to me and a large part of my time is taken up in replying. People usually don't write me unless they feel quite deeply about something. Then they unburden their heart and tell it to me like it is with them. I like it. This way we can face the need together, we can get some answers, we can come closer to God.

God has made the application of the principles of the Blessing-Pact Covenant so effective that I usually consider a letter that I receive as pre-Blessing-Pact or post-Blessing-Pact for I can tell if the person is using SEED-FAITH or not.

I can tell right away if he is putting God first. If he is, he talks about God being his Source, about giving himself, and expecting miracles from the Lord. If he knows nothing of the Blessing-Pact, he is usually still grabbing for something that will be an anchor to him.

I can also tell through the letter if the writer is living in the past or looking only to the other side, heaven. A person who is bound to the past often doesn't realize that all he talks about is what has happened to him. He hasn't the slightest idea of how to give his past to God, or to trust God for his future, and to do the most important thing of all — ENTER INTO THE NOW AND START WITH A NEW BEGINNING.

If you should meet one of our Blessing-Pact partners who is applying its principles, you will see what SEED-FAITH is really accomplishing in his life. God is with him in the most personal details of his day-to-day existence. He has discovered Jesus in a new way, not only as his personal Savior but as the Lord of his life on earth now.

CONCERN FOR BILLS

I receive hundreds of letters saying, "We didn't know before that the Lord was concerned about our bills. When we understood the Blessing-Pact, we saw Jesus in a new light. He is concerned about us, especially with the bills we have to pay."

Not long ago, a family wrote, "For the first time we have plenty to eat." Living in a ghettolike area where nobody seems to know that Jesus wants to meet them at the point of their needs, they had accepted what they thought was their fate: being hungry all the time. The idea of SEED-FAITH caught fire in their hearts and right where food is the scarcest God supplied their needs.

A DOCTOR DISCOVERS A RIOT AREA COULDN'T DEFEAT HIM

A doctor whose office was in a ghetto area saw his practice go down and down. Other doctors moved out. He wrote, "My office was located where some of the riots were happening. I felt impressed to stay It was rough going. The building we were in was hit, but not our office. The worst thing was the fear in the neighborhood. It affected our business. Even those who needed our services couldn't always pay. We got our eyes opened through the Blessing-Pact and found that it's not necessarily the physical location but where we are in terms of our relationship with God. We learned that God indeed is THE Source and that as we give to Him, He gives to us.

"All through the summer of riots we kept up our giving. It wasn't always easy to expect a miracle, especially when we looked at the natural sight around us. But we looked to God, to the SEED-FAITH we were sowing, and continued doing all we could for our clients, whether they had money or not. It was this that enabled us to expect a miracle. It came. When it was no longer possible to stay where we were, a lovely new office opened, we moved in, and soon doubled our practice. We keep Oral Roberts' literature in the reception room. People are always asking what we have that's so different. My wife told several about our Blessing-Pact. They said, 'Tell us how we can join.' Now the Blessing-Pact is working for them. Christ has come right down into our place of business and given us guidance. He is our Lord and Savior. We are thrilled to have our Blessing-Pact with Him. It has made the difference in us spiritually and financially."

HOW CAN I PAY MY DEBTS?

In this so-called affluent country where there is so much, many people have problems that have taken all their earnings and thrown them hopelessly in debt. Because of this some have lost the desire to try to pay their debts. Others have schemed to find ways to avoid paying.

I love to help people like this understand the principles of SEED-FAITH and start getting honest with God, themselves, and the people they deal with.

Take this letter: "I am behind in my payments, still, the bills continue to pile up. I can never catch up. I don't see why I have to pay these debts anyway."

I replied, "Paying your debts is a scriptural obligation. You must not think you can be blessed if you have no determination to be paying on your bills. This is contrary to God's law of putting Him first in your life. It violates the principle of giving and receiving. It simply will not work. It is bad seed, which, if you continue to sow, will multiply back to you more bills and more debts.

"But when you pay on your bills you are sowing good seed. Seed that God will multiply back to help those who carry you on their books, and back to you with more funds to meet every bill and on time!

"You must pay your bills so that your heart will not condemn you. The Bible says, 'If our heart condemn us not, then have we confidence toward God' (1 John 3:21).

"You must pay your bills for the sake of your witness for Christ.

"The Blessing-Pact, by helping you look to God as THE Source of supply for your bills will give you confidence that He will provide the means to pay these bills."

Nearly every day I receive letters from Blessing-Pact partners who tell of collecting on bad debts. Here's a recent one:

Dear Brother Roberts:

I joined the Blessing-Pact in June. Along with other things I asked prayer for finances. We had several outstanding debts; two customers had owed us way over a year. They said the equipment we put in their boats worked fine, but they turned a deaf ear to our pleas for them to pay the bills. But on August 21, customer number 1 sent me a check for $1,184.89. On August 30, customer number 2 paid the $71.75 he had owed so long.

I know it was God for we had tried so many times to collect and had failed.

Mrs. L. B. W., Florida

A friend of mine for years, owner of a garage, had given up on some people who owed him. Even though he had the Blessing-Pact he still could not believe for these bad debts. Then one day a new understanding of his Blessing-Pact dawned. He said, "I've put in SEED-FAITH by paying my debts, even when it was hard to do. Now I know God will multiply this seed I have sown, back to me. Somebody is going to pay me soon."

Soon here came a letter: "Dear Oral Roberts: It's true what you say about God multiplying SEED-FAITH." Then he told of standing on Philippians 4:19, "But my God shall supply all your need..." He said, "Two persons came in and paid their past-due accounts. One I had charged off 25 years ago, and the other one two years ago! PRAISE GOD!"

You see, when your heart doesn't condemn you, and you know you are looking to God, and when you love Him and are giving to Him, you can use your Blessing-Pact for specific things.

HOW CAN I GIVE WHEN I DON'T HAVE ANY MONEY?

This is what a man said to me as he faced bankruptcy. I felt God would deliver him from his financial strain if he would start giving. He said he didn't have anything left.

I said, "Everybody has something he can give. Think on it."

As he thought about it, he discovered that there was something of value he possessed which could be converted into money later. I said, "Tell God two things, 'I'll do it, and I'll expect a miracle.'"

He replied, "But I've never had a miracle."

"Oh, yes, you have," I answered. "When you received Christ as your personal Savior and God saved your soul, that was a miracle. In the same way God can give you a miracle in your finances. He tells you to give and you shall receive. Therefore, as you give this, expect a miracle."

Remember: God wouldn't tell you to give, if you had nothing to give.

Remember: God wouldn't tell you to give, if He didn't intend for you to receive.

Remember: God wouldn't tell you to give, if He didn't plan to use it to help others and multiply it back to meet your needs.

Remember: God doesn't play with something as important as your life!

In addition to the letters I receive from people in general, I receive a great many from young people. Here is one from a 17-year-old boy who saw our TV Special, CONTACT, and wrote me:

Dear Oral Roberts:

I am 17 years old and my father is a minister. I am what the press would call a hippie. But really, I am just trying to find what life really is.

This summer I tripped on LSD and ever since then I have been filled with fear and frustration and depression, and I am really lost. I also used an excess of "speed" this summer. I have been going downhill ever since I quit school last year.

I have always trusted and believed in God and I know God has the power to bring me out of this nightmare. So please help me. I have learned the hard way that LSD is nothing to play with. I really believe that through you, God can heal me, so please help me.

God bless you for your prayer.

Your lost friend,
Mike

P.S. I want something good to happen to me.

Here is my reply to him:

My dear Mike:

I've just returned home and found your letter waiting. I am so glad you wrote to me. As I read your letter I felt your soul was reaching out to God. There is real hope for your salvation.

Mike, I was a preacher's son and exactly your same age of 17 when I took "my trip" — not on drugs but on my rebellion against my parents, against the church, and against society in general. Perhaps, as you say, it might have been that I was trying to find what life really is.

What I found, Mike, was that I was sowing seed — seed of rebellion against God who had been trying to draw me to himself and give me real life. Each seed I sowed was multiplied back, but it was not the harvest I had expected. It was multiplied back in frustration, loneliness, fear, and eventually sickness that put me to bed for five months and almost took my life.

You indicated that the LSD seed you sowed has been multiplied back as frustration, fear, depression — and desperation. The one Book in the world that is absolutely true is the Bible. In the Bible,

God says, "Whatsoever a man soweth, that shall he also reap." You see through your own experience that all of life is sowing and reaping. You have proved the Bible to be true, for each seed you have sown has resulted in this bad harvest which has now left you in this nightmare.

I am proud of you for making this confession. God says, "If we confess our sins, he is faithful and just to forgive our sins, and to cleanse us from all unrighteousness" (1 John 1:9).

I am also proud that you recognize God is real, and has power to deliver you. I am proud you have written for the prayers of a man of God.

Yes, Mike, God can help you and here's how to make your covenant with Him for a new life.

FIRST, START LOOKING TO GOD AS THE SOURCE OF YOUR SUPPLY. The Bible says, "But my God shall supply all your need according to his riches in glory by Christ Jesus" (Philippians 4:19). God is THE Source of your supply — of finding life's meaning — of receiving peace of soul and mind — of receiving power for a successful life. God is the Source — not LSD, or speed, or any other thing, or any other person.

SECOND, THE LIFE-STYLE OF JESUS WAS GIVING. HE SAID, "GIVE, AND IT SHALL BE GIVEN UNTO YOU..." (Luke 6:38). The Cross of Christ is really a Person, Jesus Christ, who gave himself. He gave up all rights to himself, submitting His own will to God, saying, "Father, not my will but thine be done."

He gave so much — He gave of His riches becoming poor for our sakes that we might be rich in all good things. He gave of His love, His faith, His talent, His time, His touch. He said, "I came not to be ministered unto but to give..." Jesus gave as seed, each gift was a seed planted to be multiplied back, each seed planted was the basis on which He received back.

Now you experimented with drugs to GET, not to give. I've done this thing of trying to GET, too, and you and I know it doesn't work. You can't receive by GETTING; you receive by giving. The hole you give through is the hole you receive through.

Start giving. Each act of giving is seed you are sowing for God to multiply back to you in the form of your need. Read John 6:1-13 of how a young lad merely gave Christ his lunch — five little loaves and two fishes. Christ took it, blessed and broke it, and multiplied it into 5,000 meals for that many hungry men — THEN returned it to the boy 12 TIMES PLUS. Jesus still works this way. When we give, even the tiniest seed is often multiplied 5,000 times. Look at any tree and remember how small the seed was that somebody planted.

You receive through your giving. Only what we give can God multiply back to us. If you give nothing, even if God multiplies it, it is still nothing.

Start giving, Mike — some of your talent, your money, your time, your love, your faith, your helping hand. Then watch and see God multiply it back to meet your deepest needs.

Finally, in making your covenant with God, start expecting a miracle.

You wrote for my prayers and I have already

started praying for you. I'm also asking the students and faculty of Oral Roberts University to pray. God will hear our prayers. But — and this is very important to you — you must have evidence for your own faith to be released toward God. That evidence is STARTING TO LOOK TO GOD AS YOUR SOURCE, AND STARTING TO GIVE AS SEED FOR A HARVEST OF LIFE TO BE RETURNED TO YOU. When you know in your heart that you are trusting God as THE Source, your Savior and Lord, your Supply for every need — when you know in your heart that you are *giving* — then, as we pray with you, you have a solid basis on which to expect God to send you a miracle: a miracle for your deliverance in soul, mind, body, and all your other needs in this life.

This is what I call the BLESSING-PACT COVENANT WITH GOD. It is the scriptural plan God is using to help people through this ministry. It really works if you work it. Thousands are being changed by it.

Sorry to write such a long letter but your letter touched my heart and I know there are no easy answers. God's answer involves your whole life. Are you ready to give it to Him to multiply back to you with a new life that is more abundant?

Let's pray: "O God, I am sorry for my sins. Forgive me and give me a new start. You are now my Source of supply. I will start giving of my total self, and I am expecting a miracle. In Jesus' name, Amen."

I am sending you some literature. God bless it to your needs.

Bye for now. Write me again real soon. I am concerned with your needs being met. God bless you and He does. Something good is going to happen to you — today!

Your partner always,
Oral Roberts

In a recent chapel service at ORU I read Mike's letter and my answer to him (keeping his last name confidential.)

A student heard me read the two letters without having the benefit of reading them herself and having time to digest what I said in my reply.

She was kind enough to write me the following letter:

Dear President Roberts,

I'm expecting a great year here at ORU. This is my third year here — I'm a returning junior.

The chapels have improved greatly over the last few years. This morning's chapel was no exception. I could tell in my spirit — as I'm sure the rest of the student body could — that Mike's need was a desperate one. Your reply letter started out very well by identifying with the same searching feeling in your own teen years.

I agreed with the first part of the letter about his recognizing his need. Then you stated, "How can he *receive* if he always tries to *get*." According to the Bible, which you brought out, one must give in order to receive. What a person gives and what he receives is the issue. A person, I think, should give himself — meaning his soul — to the Lord in order to *receive* SALVATION.

I don't know whether I just misunderstood the

letter or what, but it seemed to me your emphasis was on giving money in order to receive. The thought that hit me as soon as you said "Blessing-Pact" was *Is this a form of indulgence? Will Mike get the idea that he has to give money in order to receive peace?*

I talked this over with two of my girl friends — who are from different denominational backgrounds than I — they felt the same way.

If you recognize my name it's because I'm a Blessing-Pact partner. I'm using it mainly as a means to give more to the Lord. I realize different people use it in different ways. But don't you think it's possible for a misunderstanding of its use to develop?

Not only Mike, but countless others, could be using it as a *type of indulgence*. In that they give only to receive could be disastrous if they don't give their heart too.

This is one part of the Blessing-Pact that I'm uncertain about. Should our philosophy be to give in order to receive?

I would appreciate your reply.

Sincerely,
Carol

Here is part of my reply to her:

Dear Carol:

One of the greatest services that we have been able to render to people in our day is to give them a point of contact for the releasing of their faith. Yes, there is a danger that people will misunderstand some aspects of the Blessing-Pact. But there is also a danger that people will misunderstand in every area of life. The greatest danger of all is that people will do nothing to encourage the releasing of their faith.

You tell people to give themselves to God, or to believe in Christ, and the hang-up is — how, how do you do it? The greatest success that we have had in bringing people to God is to give them a point of contact for the releasing of their faith.

Remember this, a point of contact is something you do, that when you do it, it helps you to believe. Our point of contact with water is turning a faucet; with electricity, flipping a switch; with our automobile, turning a key in the lock to engage the starter.

Because of the simplicity of the point of contact, many people do nothing and receive nothing. Many people have misunderstood our encouragement to touch the radio or the TV and to lay their hands on the body or some other very simple point of contact. The reason they refuse to do one of these things is because they misunderstood, while others did this relatively simple thing and it encouraged them to believe God for their miracle.

You will notice that every promise of God's is a conditional thing. The finders are the seekers, the door-openers are the knockers, and the receivers are those who pray. Also, Jesus said it shall be given unto you on the condition of your giving.

There is nothing wrong with giving that you may receive, because all of life is premised on this fact. When people receive who do not give, they do not appreciate it or they do not usually know how to use it.

This is why the Blessing-Pact has been such great encouragement to so many, while others have misunderstood it and will continue to misunderstand it. It will not hinder those who are able to appreciate and use it for the glory of God and their goal.

Of course, there are many wonderful points of contact with God's power, including searching the Scriptures, praying, Holy Communion, praying for others, and so forth. You see, we project this philosophy by:

1. Teaching the fact that God is our Source.
2. Giving your best to Him that you may receive His best.
3. Using the Blessing-Pact as a point of contact to release your faith and expect a miracle.

I hope this letter is a blessing to you and to those with whom you have been talking. Please write me again soon. God bless you for your interest in this ministry and may your Blessing-Pact partnership encourage a greater fulfillment in every area of your life.

Your Partner,
Oral Roberts

What I wanted Carol to see in my reply to her letter is that giving is more than giving your soul to the Lord for salvation. This is, of course, the greatest miracle of all. But it must not stop there.

Like many persons, Carol was picking out what she wanted to hear or had been preconditioned or taught all her life to hear. She thought when I mentioned *giving*, that I was referring only to money. But I didn't stop there. What I told Mike was this: "Give some of your talent, your money, your time, your love, your faith, your helping hand. Then watch God multiply it back to meet your deepest needs."

Now, I would like for you to read again my answer to Mike. Read it slowly and prayerfully. It sums up the three key principles of the Blessing-Pact and tells how to make it work in your own life for your specific needs.

I am going to close this book just as I started it. Jesus comes to you at the point of your need. Through Him, as your Source, that need can be met.

The life-style of Jesus was giving. Through learning to give of your total self, you are sowing SEED-FAITH, and you can, therefore, confidently expect a miracle from our Lord.

I have lived these key principles for many years in my personal relationship with Jesus Christ, and they work. As I have written them down in this book, I have relived these experiences. They have brought a new glory in my heart and I feel a new exhilaration as I have shared these principles with you that have changed my life and the lives of thousands of others, including members of my family.

Now I want you to remember: Look to God as your Source. Put God first in your life and in your giving. Then expect a miracle and the Blessing-Pact Covenant will work for you. Bring your believing to a culmination by saying, "I'll do it and I'll expect a miracle!"

I have said it before; I say it again: It always works when you work it!

SOMETHING GOOD IS GOING TO HAPPEN TO YOU!

Dear Friend,

My prayer for you is that MIRACLE OF SEED FAITH will help you learn that God is greater than any problem you have. But, I want to go beyond that. I want to pray for you personally. So, I invite you to write me and tell me your prayer request. I promise I'll pray and I'll write you back. Simply address your letter:

Oral Roberts
Tulsa, Oklahoma   74171

If you have a special prayer request, you are encouraged to call the Abundant Life Prayer Group at (918-492-7777). Call anytime, day or night, and a trained prayer partner will answer your call and pray with you.

Oral Roberts

CHRISTIAN HERITAGE Readers Club Inc.

River Hills Plantation
Clover, S.C. 29710

We hope you enjoyed this book... normally you would have paid $3.95 for it...but because of our, "Reprint rights," it costs you considerably less!

If you want to read more good inspirational books like this, we have good news for you. We have developed a, **"Dollar Book Club."** Turn the page for complete details.

The "Dollar Book Club"

A New Concept.

Here's three simple rules explaining how it works:
1) The Annual membership is just $5.00. When you join we send you, FREE BONUS BOOKS with a retail value of $12.90.

FREE BOOKS FOR JOINING OUR CLUB

Hard Cover, Red Letter, Dictionary Concordance Your name embossed in gold.

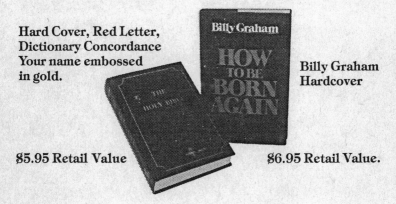

Billy Graham Hardcover

$5.95 Retail Value

$6.95 Retail Value.

2) We'll send you a catalog, four times a year — April, June, September and November. Offering you hundreds of books with Retail Value to: $8.95 for just $1.00 each. Plus a small postage & handling charge.

3) You can buy as many books as you like...You are only required to purchase ONE book to keep your membership active!

The membership form is on the back page. Just turn the page and fill it out.

I want to join
The "Dollar Book Club"

Charge my membership to:

( ) Visa/Master Charge# _____

_____Exp. Date:_____

( ) Bill me, 30 day terms.

( ) I enclose check or money order.

Rush my Bible and Hardcover Bonus Books to:

Name: _____

Address: _____

_____Zip_____

Name to be embossed on FREE Bible (Please Print)

_____

    I agree to the following terms and conditions:
To pay the annual membership fee and to purchase one book for $1.00 from your catalog sent to me in, April, June, September and November. Should I not order, my membership will automatically be subject, without notice, to cancellation, without refund of any portion of the membership fee.

    I have read the terms and conditions of this agreement and my signature constitutes acceptance of these terms and conditions:

_____
Signature

I didn't hear any more for this turned me off completely. *Patient,* I thought, *being patient is not going to cure my lungs of tuberculosis.* What I needed was someone to show me the living Christ who wouldn't say, "Son, be patient," but would say, "Son, rise, take up thy bed and walk."

EVERYONE HAS NEEDS

One cannot work with the thousands who have sought help through the instrumentality of this ministry without seeing that everybody has needs.

Those needs are not always the same. But everybody is sick in some way. Particularly is this true when <u>sickness is defined</u> as it was <u>by Jesus as disharmony</u>. Seldom is a person found who is at one with God, himself, and other people. Nor do you often see a person at harmony in his spirit, mind, and body. He is out of adjustment. Either his body is out of harmony with his soul, or his mind is in conflict with his body, or his soul is in harmony and his mind and body are not. It is in this way that much of sickness takes form.

Therefore, the whole man needs healing. The only Man in history who talked about making a person whole is Jesus Christ. He came to heal the whole man — body, mind, and soul — and to give him a harmony within himself.

It is at a point of need that Jesus comes to every person and awakens his interest. He awakens his interest in the life He brings: abundant life here and life eternal.

Jesus made it very clear that He had come to heal man, to bring forth his talents, to open up his inner man to giving and loving, to show him how to believe and use his faith, how to take authority over his problems and needs, and how to sow that he might reap.

JESUS' RELATIONSHIP WITH YOUR NEEDS

My experience has taught me that no man will fully fol-

11 HOW CHRIST APPEARS TO YOU IN THE FORM OF YOUR NEED

I CAN NEVER BE GRATEFUL ENOUGH for the understanding I have gained of Jesus, concerning the way He comes to a person at a <u>point</u> of his need, in the <u>form</u> of that need, and to <u>meet</u> that need according to His riches.

Mahatma Gandhi said, "Not even God would dare to appear to a hungry man except in the form of bread."

I once studied Jesus and His life as written in the Four Gospels — Matthew, Mark, Luke, and John — until I committed to memory His every recorded incident and most of His sayings. I became so absorbed that I felt as if I were living with the Man. I've had that feeling ever since.

As I have already indicated, Jesus came to me in the form of my need which was for healing. When I learned that He was concerned about me as I was in that moment, I began listening. God got my attention.

Knowing my makeup, I seriously doubt that I would ever have surrendered my life to Christ had I not understood He had first come to me in the form of my healing.

I recall during my illness a minister called on me. He was extremely sympathetic and gracious. He tried to comfort me. In the prayer he offered I heard him say, "Lord, help this boy to be patient in his illness."

HOW YOU CAN COMPREHEND GOD

Neither in himself nor in trusting to some other power
can a man's basic needs be met. When he begins to realize
that his needs are not being met, this is a great moment. For
it is through his needs that he can begin to comprehend God.

The Holy Spirit gives him light and understanding about
God's sending His Son into the world to give him life more
abundantly. The Spirit brings conviction to his heart that
he has been following his own way, and the way of other
forces, to his own hurt and destruction, and that only through
Christ can he live.

As you begin to listen to the gospel of good news, Jesus
Christ is brought to you in the form of your needs. Then you
see Christ as THE answer — and LIFE itself.

Jesus Christ is rest for your soul.
Jesus Christ is peace for your inner man.
Jesus Christ is light for your path.
Jesus Christ is bread for your hunger.
Jesus Christ is healing for your whole being.
Jesus Christ is the supply for all your needs.
Jesus Christ is God's will for your life.
Jesus Christ is the hope of your existence.
Jesus Christ is the beginning and end of your faith.
Jesus Christ is the solution of your problems.
Jesus Christ is the form of your every need.

When you become aware of your needs, and of Christ's
being the answer to your needs, almost invariably you will
choose to accept Christ as your Lord and Master.

The reason so many don't is that Christ has not been
fully presented. Jesus said, "And I, if I be lifted up from the
earth, will draw all men unto me" (John 12:32).

I have seen 5,000 men accept Christ in less than an hour